Pulled Beef Sandwiches

I'VE HAD THIS RECIPE SINCE I WAS A NEWLYWED. EVEN PEOPLE WHO DISLIKE CABBAGE LOVE THIS. LONG SIMMERING MAKES THE CABBAGE DISAPPEAR INTO THE BEEF, CREATING GREAT FLAVOR AND TEXTURE.

SIDE: Sweet and Sour Coleslaw (page 179).

DESSERT: No-Bake Chocolate Cookies (page 227).

MAKES: 24 sandwiches

- 4 pounds cooked roast beef, shredded
- 9 cups shredded cabbage
- 2 cups ketchup
- 1 15-ounce can beef broth
- ¾ cup Worcestershire sauce
- 2 tablespoons freshly squeezed lemon juice
- 1 tablespoon yellow mustard
- 2 teaspoons salt (or to taste)
- 24 hamburger buns

ONE In a 4- to 6-quart Dutch oven combine shredded beef, cabbage, ketchup, beef broth, Worcestershire sauce, lemon juice, mustard, and salt.

TWO Cover and simmer over low heat for 1 hour, stirring occasionally. Uncover and simmer for 1 hour more, stirring occasionally. Serve on buns.

PLAN AHEAD: Prepare up to 3 days ahead. Cover and refrigerate. Reheat over low heat.

FREEZE AHEAD: Place all ingredients, except hamburger buns, in a freezer bag and freeze up to 2 months. Defrost completely in refrigerator. Continue according to Step Two.

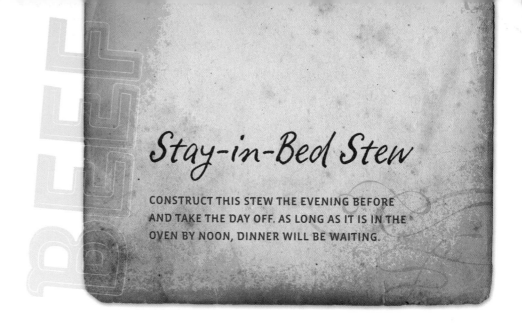

Stay-in-Bed Stew

CONSTRUCT THIS STEW THE EVENING BEFORE AND TAKE THE DAY OFF. AS LONG AS IT IS IN THE OVEN BY NOON, DINNER WILL BE WAITING.

SIDES: Parmesan Toast (page 163) and Blue Cheese Wedge Salad (page 200).

DESSERT: Purchased ice cream sandwiches.

MAKES: 6 servings

- 2 pounds beef stew meat
- 4 medium potatoes, peeled and cut into 1-inch pieces
- 4 carrots, cut into 1-inch pieces
- 3 stalks celery, cut into 1-inch pieces
- 1 large onion, sliced
- 1 cup sliced fresh mushrooms
- 1 teaspoon salt
- ½ teaspoon black pepper
- 1 24-ounce can hot-style vegetable juice

ONE Preheat oven to 275°F.

TWO In a 4- to 6-quart Dutch oven layer stew meat, potatoes, carrots, celery, onion, and mushrooms; sprinkle with salt and pepper. Pour vegetable juice over all. Bake, uncovered, about 5 hours or until hot and bubbly.

FREEZE AHEAD: Place cooked stew in a freezer bag and freeze up to 2 months. Defrost completely in refrigerator. Reheat over medium heat until hot and bubbly.

Beef and Veggie Five-Spice Stir-Fry

TRY THIS GREAT WAY TO GET KIDS TO EAT VEGETABLES.

SIDES: Steamed rice, cooked Asian noodles, or vermicelli noodles.

DESSERT: Loaf pound cake served with assorted mixed berries.

MAKES: 8 to 10 servings

- 2 **pounds boneless beef sirloin steak**
- 1 **tablespoon hoisin sauce**
- 1 **tablespoon soy sauce**
- 1 **teaspoon Chinese five-spice powder**
- 2 **tablespoons seasoned stir-fry oil or vegetable oil**
- 3 **cups fresh snow peas, trimmed**
- 1 **15-ounce can baby corn, drained**
- 2 **medium carrots, thinly sliced**
- 1 **large onion, cut into 1-inch pieces (1½ to 2 cups)**
- 2 **14-ounce cans beef broth**
- 2 **tablespoons cornstarch**

ONE If desired, place meat in freezer until partially frozen for easier slicing. Trim fat from meat. Thinly slice meat across the grain into bite-size strips.

TWO Place beef strips in a resealable plastic bag; add hoisin sauce, soy sauce, and five-spice powder. Seal bag; turn to coat evenly. Refrigerate meat for 1 to 12 hours.

THREE Preheat oil in a wok or large skillet over high heat. Add beef strips, half at a time, to hot wok. Stir-fry for 2 to 3 minutes or until to desired doneness. Remove beef strips from wok. Add snow peas, baby corn, carrot, and onion to hot wok. Stir-fry about 3 minutes or until onion begins to often. Return beef strips to wok. Add 1½ cans of the beef broth to wok; bring to boiling.

FOUR Meanwhile, whisk cornstarch into the remaining ½ can beef broth; add to wok and stir until thickened.

PLAN AHEAD: Prepare through Step Two up to 12 hours ahead. Continue according to Step Three.

Eye of Round Roast

MAKE THIS DISH FOR AN ELEGANT COMPANY DINNER OR SPECIAL FAMILY MEAL.

SIDE: Apple-Walnut-Raisin Spinach Salad (page 197).

DESSERT: Chocolate Pecan Pie (page 240) with ice cream.

MAKES: 6 to 8 servings

- 1 4-pound eye of round beef roast
- 2 cups finely chopped onion
- 1 cup red wine vinegar
- ½ cup molasses
- 4 to 6 cloves garlic, minced
- 2 bay leaves

ONE Place roast in a resealable plastic bag set in a deep bowl. For marinade, combine onion, vinegar, molasses, garlic, and bay leaves. Pour marinade over meat; seal bag. Refrigerate 8 hours or overnight, turning bag several times.

TWO Preheat oven to 325°F. Place roast and marinade in a shallow baking dish; cover loosely with foil. Bake about 2 hours or until internal temperature reads 135°F, basting with marinade every 30 minutes. Remove bay leaves.

THREE Let meat stand 5 minutes. To serve, cut meat into thin slices. Drizzle with hot marinade.

FREEZE AHEAD: Place roast and marinade in a freezer bag and freeze up to 2 months. Defrost completely in refrigerator. Continue according to Step Two.

Orange Beef and Broccoli Stir-Fry

ORANGE MARMALADE GIVES A KICK TO THE BEEF AND BROCCOLI.

SIDES: Steamed rice, hot and sour soup.

DESSERT: Miracle Pecan-Caramel Bars (page 226).

MAKES: 8 servings

1½	pounds beef skirt steak or flank steak
1	cup orange marmalade
¼	cup hoisin sauce
3	tablespoons teriyaki sauce
2	tablespoons soy sauce
1	tablespoon minced fresh garlic
12	ounces fresh broccoli florets

ONE If desired, place meat in freezer until partially frozen for easier slicing. Trim fat from meat. Thinly slice meat across the grain into bite-size strips.

TWO In a large bowl toss together beef strips, marmalade, hoisin sauce, teriyaki sauce, soy sauce, and garlic.

THREE In a medium saucepan cook broccoli in boiling water 5 to 6 minutes until crispy tender; drain and cool.

FOUR Preheat a wok or large nonstick skillet over high heat. Add meat mixture to hot wok. Stir-fry for 4 to 6 minutes or to desired doneness. Add cooked broccoli, heat through.

FREEZE AHEAD: Place all ingredients, except broccoli, in a freezer bag and freeze up to 2 months. Defrost completely in refrigerator. Add broccoli and continue according to Step Three.

Asian Flank Steak

THE SECRET TO A TENDER, JUICY STEAK IS TO TAKE IT OFF THE HEAT MEDIUM RARE AND THINLY SLICE IT ACROSS THE GRAIN. THIS SWEET AND ZESTY MARINADE IS PERFECT FOR A HEARTY STEAK.

SIDE: Blue Cheese Wedge Salad (page 200).

DESSERT: Shortbread and butter pecan ice cream.

MAKES: 6 to 8 servings

- 1 2- to 2½-pound beef flank steak
- ½ cup soy sauce
- ¼ cup freshly squeezed lemon juice
- ¼ cup finely minced onion
- ¼ cup packed brown sugar
- 2 tablespoons toasted sesame oil
- 1 tablespoon grated fresh ginger
- 1 tablespoon minced fresh garlic
- 1 teaspoon dried red pepper flakes (optional)

ONE Place flank steak in a resealable plastic bag; add soy sauce, lemon juice, onion, brown sugar, sesame oil, ginger, garlic, and, if desired, red pepper flakes. Seal bag; turn to coat evenly. Refrigerate 1 to 24 hours, turning bag occasionally.

TWO Preheat grill to medium-high heat.

THREE Remove steak from bag, reserving marinade. Grill for 10 to 16 minutes for medium rare (135°F), turning once halfway through grilling. Meanwhile, simmer marinade over medium heat until reduced by half; keep warm.

FOUR Let steak stand 5 minutes. To serve, slice meat across the grain into very thin slices. Drizzle with reduced marinade.

FREEZE AHEAD: Add all ingredients to a freezer bag and freeze up to 1 month. Defrost completely in refrigerator. Continue according to Step Two.

Beef and Vegetable Soup

BESIDES THE ROUND STEAK, THE TWO "MUST-HAVE" INGREDIENTS IN THIS SOUP ARE THE CANNED TOMATOES AND ONION. TOGETHER, THEY CREATE A TASTY BLEND, GIVING THE SOUP AN OLD-FASHIONED, HEARTY FLAVOR.

SIDE: Green Chile and Cheese Corn Bread (page 164).

DESSERT: Chocolate Sheet Cake with Chocolate Icing (page 246).

MAKES: 8 servings

- 1   pound beef round steak
- 1   teaspoon seasoned salt
- 2   tablespoons vegetable oil
- 4   cups water
- 1   28-ounce can chopped tomatoes, undrained
- 1   15-ounce can green beans, undrained
- 1   15-ounce can white kidney beans, undrained
- 1½ cups chopped onion
- 1½ cups sliced celery
- 1   cup frozen corn
- 1   cup sliced carrot
- 1   teaspoon salt (or to taste)
- 1   teaspoon dried Italian mixed herbs, crushed
- 1   bay leaf

ONE Trim fat from steak; cut into 1-inch pieces. Sprinkle with seasoned salt.

TWO Preheat oil in a 4- to 6-quart Dutch oven or soup pot. Add steak pieces and brown on all sides. Stir in water, undrained tomatoes, undrained green beans, undrained kidney beans, onion, celery, corn, carrot, salt, Italian herbs, and bay leaf.

THREE Cover and simmer gently for 35 to 45 minutes. Remove bay leaf before serving.

PLAN AHEAD: Prepare up to 4 days ahead. Cover and refrigerate. Reheat over medium heat until hot and bubbly.

FREEZE AHEAD: Place cooked soup in a freezer bag and freeze up to 2 months. Defrost completely in refrigerator. Reheat over medium heat until hot and bubbly.

Beef Fajitas

JUST SAYING "FAJITAS" MAKES IT A PARTY. KEEP A SERAPE TO USE AS A TABLECLOTH ON FAJITA NIGHT.

SIDES: Sour cream, guacamole, shredded lettuce, chopped tomatoes, sliced green onions, and sliced fresh jalapeño chile peppers.

DESSERT: Instant Sopaipillas (page 231).

MAKES: 6 to 8 servings

- 1   1¼- to 1½-pound beef skirt steak or flank steak
- ¼   cup freshly squeezed lime juice
- ¼   cup olive oil
- 2   tablespoons chili powder
- 2   cups sliced onion
- 2   cups sliced bell pepper
- 1   teaspoon salt
- ½   teaspoon black pepper
- 12   6-inch flour tortillas

ONE Place steak in a resealable plastic bag. For marinade, whisk together lime juice, 2 tablespoons of the oil, and chili powder; add to bag. Seal bag; turn to coat evenly. Refrigerate for 2 to 12 hours.

TWO Remove steak from bag, reserving marinade. Preheat grill to medium-high heat. Grill steak for 10 to 16 minutes for medium rare (135°F), turning once halfway through grilling. Remove steak from grill; keep warm.

THREE Meanwhile, preheat the remaining 2 tablespoons oil in a large skillet over medium-high heat; add chili powder, onion, and bell pepper. Cook and stir until tender. Season with salt and black pepper.

FOUR To serve, thinly slice meat against the grain into bite-size strips. Serve steak strips and vegetables in tortillas with sides.

PLAN AHEAD: Slice onion and bell pepper up to 1 day ahead. Refrigerate in a resealable plastic bag. Place fajita sides in bowls up to 12 hours ahead; cover and refrigerate.

FREEZE AHEAD: Place steak and marinade in a freezer bag and freeze up to 2 months. Defrost completely in refrigerator. Continue according to Step Two.

Lemon-Ginger London Broil

LEMON AND GINGER NOT ONLY GIVE ZESTY FLAVOR TO THIS STEAK, THEY ALSO HELP TENDERIZE IT. SLICED STEAK IS GREAT LEFTOVER, SERVED ON A SALAD.

SIDES: Sesame Chop Chop Salad (page 178) and Pecan Wild Rice Pilaf (page 154).

DESSERT: Ice Cream Snowballs: Form ice cream balls with an ice cream scoop; roll in shredded coconut and freeze on a parchment-lined baking sheet. Serve on a puddle of chocolate sauce.

MAKES: 6 to 8 servings

- 1 2- to 2½-pound beef flank steak
- ½ cup freshly squeezed lemon juice
- 2 tablespoons lemon zest
- 2 tablespoons olive oil
- 2 tablespoons grated fresh ginger
- 1 tablespoon minced fresh garlic
- 1 teaspoon black pepper

ONE Place flank steak in a resealable plastic bag. Add lemon juice, lemon zest, oil, ginger, garlic, and pepper. Seal bag; turn to coat evenly. Refrigerate for 12 to 24 hours, turning bag occasionally.

TWO Preheat grill to medium-high heat.

THREE Remove steak from bag, discarding marinade. Grill for 10 to 16 minutes for medium rare (135°F), turning once halfway through grilling.

FOUR Let steak stand 5 minutes before serving. To serve, slice across the grain into very thin slices.

PLAN AHEAD: Marinate steak the night before. Prepare Asian Salad Dressing (for side) 1 day ahead; cover and refrigerate. Continue according to Step Two.

FREEZE AHEAD: Place flank steak and marinade in a freezer bag and freeze up to 2 months. Defrost completely in refrigerator. Continue according to Step Two.

Corned Beef and Cabbage

I SERVE THIS EVERY MARCH AROUND ST. PATRICK'S DAY. IT'S FUN
TO HAVE TRADITIONS THAT KIDS AND GRANDKIDS CAN ANTICIPATE.
THEY ARE LIKE ANCHORS THAT HELP TO HOLD THE FAMILY STEADY.

SIDE: Lucky Lime-and-Pineapple
Congealed Salad (page 190).

DESSERT: Mint chocolate chip
ice cream.

MAKES: 8 to 10 servings

1   3- to 4-pound marinated
     corned beef brisket

     Water

8   to 10 new potatoes

8   to 10 cabbage wedges

8   to 10 onion wedges

8   to 10 carrots, quartered

ONE Trim fat from corned beef; place in a 4- to 6-quart
Dutch oven or soup pot. Add juices and spices from
package of corned beef. Add enough water to cover
the corned beef. Cover and simmer about 2½ hours
or until almost tender, skimming foam that rises to
the top.

TWO Add potatoes, cabbage, onion, and carrot to
Dutch oven. Cover and simmer about 30 minutes
more or until vegetables are tender.

THREE Let meat stand for 10 minutes. To serve, thinly
slice meat across the grain into very thin slices. Serve
with vegetables and pan juices.

Tex-Mex Beef Fiesta

IT'S A PARTY IN YOUR MOUTH! UP THE CHILI
POWDER FOR MORE ZEST.

SIDES: Serve over corn chips with melted cheese on top, in tortilla wraps, or over packaged salad mix with salsa.

DESSERT: Vanilla ice cream with caramel sauce.

MAKES: 6 servings

1½	**pounds ground beef**
1	**cup chopped onion**
1	**cup sliced fresh mushrooms**
1	**teaspoon minced fresh garlic (or to taste)**
1	**15-ounce can diced tomatoes, undrained**
½	**cup sliced pitted black olives**
1	**tablespoon chili powder**
1	**teaspoon salt**
½	**teaspoon ground cumin**

ONE In a large skillet cook ground beef, onion, mushrooms, and garlic over medium-high heat until meat is brown. Drain off fat.

TWO Stir in undrained tomatoes, olives, chili powder, salt, and cumin. Bring to boiling. Turn heat to medium-low. Cook for 3 to 5 minutes, stirring often.

PLAN AHEAD: Prepare up to 3 days ahead. Cover and refrigerate. Reheat over medium-low heat.

FREEZE AHEAD: Place cooked meat mixture in a freezer bag and freeze up to 2 months. Defrost completely in refrigerator. Reheat over medium-low heat.

Easy Family Lasagna

DON'T BOTHER TO PREBOIL THE NOODLES. ADDING A LITTLE WATER TO THE SAUCE WILL HELP THE NOODLES COOK AS THE LASAGNA BAKES.

SIDES: Tossed green salad and Parmesan Toast (page 163).

DESSERT: Frozen Yogurt Pops (page 230).

MAKES: 12 servings

Nonstick cooking spray

- 1 pound ground beef
- ½ cup chopped onion
- 1 teaspoon dried Italian mixed herbs, crushed
- 2 26-ounce jars pasta sauce
- ½ cup water
- 6 dried lasagna noodles
- 1 16-ounce container cottage cheese
- ½ cup grated Parmesan cheese
- 1 teaspoon minced fresh garlic
- 1 teaspoon dried parsley flakes
- 2 cups shredded mozzarella cheese

ONE Preheat oven to 350°F. Coat a 13×9×2-inch baking dish with cooking spray.

TWO In a large skillet cook ground beef, onion, and Italian herbs until meat is brown. Drain off fat. Stir in pasta sauce and water. Spread 1 cup of the meat mixture in the bottom of the prepared baking dish. Top with 3 uncooked noodles. Pour 2 cups of the meat mixture over the noodles.

THREE Stir together cottage cheese, Parmesan cheese, garlic, and parsley. Dollop cheese mixture on top of meat mixture and spread carefully. Top with 3 more uncooked noodles and remaining meat mixture.

FOUR Bake, uncovered, about 1 hour or until hot and bubbly. Sprinkle with mozzarella cheese. Bake 10 minutes more.

PLAN AHEAD: Prepare through Step Three up to 2 days ahead. Cover and refrigerate. Preheat oven. Uncover and continue according to Step Four.

Beef and Noodles

THIS IS ANOTHER RECIPE I MADE MANY TIMES DURING MY CHILD-REARING YEARS. MY KIDS PREFERRED AMERICAN CHEESE ON TOP, BUT, OF COURSE, ADULTS LIKE CHEDDAR.

SIDES: Buttered corn and Blue Cheese Wedge Salad (page 200).

DESSERT: Ice cream and mixed berries. (Place a bag of frozen mixed berries in the refrigerator the night before to thaw.)

MAKES: 6 servings

Nonstick cooking spray

- 1   12-ounce package dried thin egg noodles
- 1   pound ground beef
- 1   cup chopped onion
- 1   cup chopped bell pepper
- 1   teaspoon minced fresh garlic
- 1   28-ounce can chopped tomatoes, undrained
- 1   6-ounce can tomato paste
- 1   teaspoon salt
- ½   teaspoon black pepper
- 1   cup shredded cheddar cheese or 4 slices process American cheese food

ONE Preheat oven to 375°F. Coat a 2-quart casserole with cooking spray.

TWO Cook the pasta according to package directions; drain.

THREE In a large skillet cook ground beef, onion, bell pepper, and garlic until meat is brown. Drain off fat. Stir in undrained tomatoes, cooked egg noodles, tomato paste, salt, and black pepper. Spoon into prepared casserole; cover with cheese.

FOUR Bake, uncovered, about 20 minutes or until hot and bubbly.

FREEZE AHEAD: Prepare through Step Three. Cover with plastic wrap and foil. Freeze up to 2 months. Defrost completely in refrigerator. Preheat oven. Remove plastic wrap and foil and continue according to Step Four.

Cheeseburger and Fries Casserole

EVEN THE NAME SOUNDS FUN. THIS IS A CLASSIC CASSEROLE THAT KEEPS COMING BACK—ALL AGES LOVE IT.

SIDE: Cucumber-Onion Salad (page 182).

DESSERT: Cream Cheese Cupcakes (page 244).

MAKES: 8 servings

Nonstick cooking spray

- 1 pound ground beef
- 3 cups frozen potato nuggets
- 1 16-ounce can tomato sauce
- 1 cup chopped onion
- 2 teaspoons dried Italian mixed herbs, crushed
- 1 teaspoon salt
- ½ teaspoon black pepper
- 2 cups shredded cheddar cheese

ONE Preheat oven to 350°F. Coat a 13×9×2-inch baking dish with cooking spray.

TWO In a large skillet cook ground beef until brown; drain off fat.

THREE Place potato nuggets in the bottom of the prepared baking dish; top with cooked ground beef. Stir together tomato sauce, onion, Italian herbs, salt, and pepper; pour over ground beef. Sprinkle with cheese.

FOUR Bake, uncovered, about 40 minutes or until hot and bubbly.

Taco Soup

THE TORTILLAS TURN INTO LITTLE, FLAT CORN DUMPLINGS, AND TACO SEASONING GIVES JUST THE RIGHT AMOUNT OF ZEST. AT OUR HOUSE, WE PLACE A HANDFUL OF GRATED CHEDDAR CHEESE IN THE BOTTOM OF THE SOUP BOWLS BEFORE ADDING THE HOT SOUP. THE CHEESE MELTS AND THE WHOLE THING IS TO DIE FOR.

SIDES: Top with crushed corn chips, shredded cheese, and sliced green onions.

DESSERT: Instant Sopaipillas (page 231).

MAKES: 6 to 8 servings

- 2 tablespoons vegetable oil
- 6 corn tortillas, cut into 1-inch pieces
- 1 pound ground beef
- 1½ cups chopped onion
- 1 cup chopped bell pepper
- 1 teaspoon minced fresh garlic
- 2 14½-ounce cans Mexican-style diced tomatoes, undrained
- 2 14½-ounce cans water
- 1 15-ounce can small red beans, undrained
- 1 15-ounce can black beans, drained and rinsed
- 1 15-ounce can hominy, undrained, or 1½ cups frozen corn
- 1 7-ounce can diced green chile peppers, undrained
- 1 7-ounce can sliced pitted black olives, drained
- 1 1¼-ounce package taco seasoning mix

ONE Preheat oil in a 4- to 6-quart Dutch oven or soup pot. Add tortilla pieces to hot oil. Cook and stir until brown; remove and set aside. Add ground beef, onion, bell pepper, and garlic to Dutch oven. Cook until beef is brown. Drain off fat.

TWO Stir browned tortillas, undrained tomatoes, water, undrained red beans, black beans, undrained hominy, chile peppers, olives, and taco seasoning mix into Dutch oven. Bring to boiling. Turn heat to low. Simmer, uncovered, about 20 minutes, stirring occasionally.

PLAN AHEAD: Prepare up to 4 days ahead. Cover and refrigerate. Reheat over medium heat until hot and bubbly.

FREEZE AHEAD: Place cooked soup in a freezer bag and freeze up to 2 months. Defrost completely in refrigerator. Reheat over medium heat until hot and bubbly.

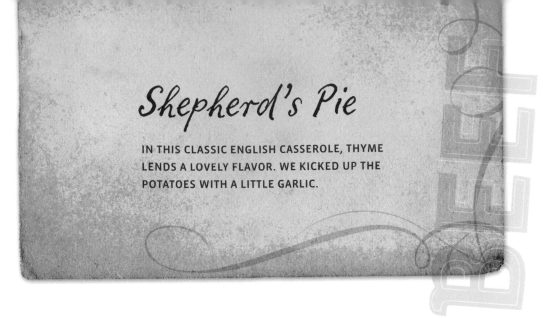

Shepherd's Pie

IN THIS CLASSIC ENGLISH CASSEROLE, THYME LENDS A LOVELY FLAVOR. WE KICKED UP THE POTATOES WITH A LITTLE GARLIC.

SIDE: Pineapple-Coconut-Carrot Salad with Coriander Dressing (page 186).

DESSERT: Apple slices and caramel dipping sauce.

MAKES: 6 servings

Nonstick cooking spray

1 pound ground beef

1 12-ounce package frozen diced onion, thawed

1 cup frozen carrots

1 cup frozen peas

1 teaspoon dried thyme, crushed

3 cups cooked mashed potatoes

1 teaspoon minced fresh garlic

1 cup shredded cheddar cheese

ONE Preheat oven to 350°F. Coat a 2-quart casserole with cooking spray.

TWO In a large skillet cook ground beef until brown; drain off fat.

THREE Stir together cooked ground beef, onion, carrots, peas, and thyme. Spoon into prepared baking dish. Stir together mashed potatoes and garlic; spread evenly over the ground beef mixture.

FOUR Bake, uncovered, for 25 minutes. Sprinkle with cheese; bake 10 minutes more.

Cranberry Sweet and Sour Meatballs

THESE MEATBALLS TOOK FIRST PLACE FOR OUR ATLANTA SUPER SUPPERS FRANCHISEE AT THE TASTE OF FORSYTH FOOD GALA AND COMPETITION.

SIDE: Tomato-Artichoke Heart Salad with Blue Cheese Dressing (page 183).

DESSERT: No-Bake Chocolate Cookies (page 227).

MAKES: 6 to 8 servings

Nonstick cooking spray

1 recipe Basic Meatballs

2 tablespoons vegetable oil

½ cup finely chopped onion

½ cup finely chopped bell pepper

1 teaspoon minced fresh garlic

1 15-ounce can jellied cranberry sauce

⅓ cup cider vinegar

⅓ cup honey

¼ cup Dijon mustard

2 tablespoons soy sauce

2 tablespoons Worcestershire sauce

½ teaspoon crushed red pepper flakes (optional)

ONE Preheat oven to 375°F. Coat a large baking sheet with cooking spray. Arrange Basic Meatballs on prepared baking sheet. Bake, uncovered, for 20 to 30 minutes or until meatballs are cooked through (internal temperature should be 160°F).

TWO Meanwhile, for sauce, preheat oil in a large saucepan over medium heat. Cook onion, bell pepper, and garlic in hot oil for 3 to 5 minutes or until onion is tender. Turn heat to low. Add cranberry sauce, vinegar, honey, mustard, soy sauce, Worcestershire sauce, and, if desired, red pepper flakes. Simmer, uncovered, for 20 minutes, stirring frequently. Add cooked meatballs; heat through.

PLAN AHEAD: Prepare through Step One up to 1 day ahead. Cover and refrigerate. Continue according to Step Two.

FREEZE AHEAD: Place cooked meatballs and sauce in a freezer bag and freeze up to 2 months. Defrost completely in refrigerator. Reheat over low heat until hot and bubbly.

BASIC MEATBALLS: In a large bowl combine ½ cup soft white bread crumbs and ½ cup milk; let soak 5 minutes. Add 2 pounds lean ground beef; ½ cup finely chopped onion; 1 egg, beaten; 1 teaspoon dried Italian mixed herbs, crushed; 1 teaspoon salt; and ½ teaspoon black pepper. Mix well. Form meat mixture into 24 large or 48 small meatballs.

Mom's Homemade Meat Loaf

JUST LIKE YOU WANT MEAT LOAF TO TASTE! WE SHOULDN'T BRAG, BUT WE THINK WE'VE PERFECTED MEAT LOAF MIX. JUST AS GOOD THE NEXT NIGHT, SLICED FOR SANDWICHES.

SIDE: Creamed Corn Casserole (page 203).

DESSERT: Strawberry Cream Cheese Angel Food Cake (page 245).

MAKES: 8 servings

Nonstick cooking spray

- 2 pounds ground beef
- 1 cup finely crushed saltine crackers
- 1 egg, beaten
- ½ cup finely chopped onion
- ½ cup finely chopped bell pepper
- ½ cup tomato sauce
- 1 tablespoon Worcestershire sauce
- 1½ teaspoons salt
- 1 teaspoon dried thyme, crushed
- ½ teaspoon black pepper
- ½ cup ketchup
- 3 slices bacon

ONE Preheat oven to 375°F. Coat a 13×9×2-inch baking dish with cooking spray.

TWO For meat loaf mixture, in a large bowl combine ground beef, crackers, egg, onion, bell pepper, tomato sauce, Worcestershire sauce, salt, thyme, and black pepper. Use a fork or your hands to mix well.

THREE Form meat loaf mixture into an 8×5×2-inch loaf in prepared baking dish. Spread ketchup over top of loaf. Place bacon slices on top.

FOUR Bake, uncovered, about 45 minutes or until internal temperature reads 155°F. Let stand 5 minutes before serving.

PLAN AHEAD: Buy ground beef in large packages since it is usually less expensive that way. Place 2-pound amounts in freezer bags and freeze up to 2 months.

FREEZE AHEAD: Place cooked meat loaf in a freezer bag and freeze up to 2 months. Defrost in refrigerator. To reheat, preheat oven to 300°F. Place meat loaf in baking dish. Bake, covered, for 20 to 30 minutes or until internal temperature reads 155°F.

MOM'S HOMEMADE BARBECUED MEAT LOAF: Prepare as directed, except substitute barbecue sauce for the tomato sauce in the meat loaf mixture and for the ketchup on top of the loaf.

Stuffed Bell Peppers

THIS DISH IS BEAUTIFUL; JUST LOOKING AT IT GETS
EVERYONE EXCITED ABOUT DINNER.

SIDES: Chef Duane's Spanish Rice (page 158) and chilled sliced fruit.

DESSERT: Chocolate Pecan Pie (page 240).

MAKES: 6 servings

Nonstick cooking spray

3 large bell peppers

1 recipe Mom's Homemade Meat Loaf mixture (page 37)

1 recipe Basic Marinara Sauce

ONE Preheat oven to 375°F. Coat a 13×9×2-inch baking dish with cooking spray.

TWO Cut each bell pepper in half lengthwise, cutting through the middle of the stem. Remove the seeds and filaments but not the stem.

THREE Divide the meat loaf mixture evenly among the bell pepper halves, pressing mixture into peppers and forming a mound on top. Place the filled peppers in prepared baking dish. Pour the Basic Marinara Sauce evenly over the filled peppers.

FOUR Bake, uncovered, about 45 minutes or until internal temperature of the meat mixture reads 155°F.

PLAN AHEAD: Prepare through Step Three up to 1 day ahead. Cover and refrigerate. Preheat oven. Uncover and continue according to Step Four.

FREEZE AHEAD: Prepare through Step Three. Place filled peppers in a freezer container and freeze up to 2 months. Defrost completely in refrigerator. Preheat oven. Place peppers in baking dish. Continue according to Step Four.

BASIC MARINARA SAUCE: In a medium saucepan combine one 28-ounce can chopped tomatoes undrained; ½ cup finely chopped onion; ½ cup finely chopped bell pepper; 1 tablespoon tomato paste; 1 teaspoon minced fresh garlic; and 1 teaspoon dried Italian mixed herbs, crushed. Bring to boiling over medium heat. Reduce heat and simmer about 20 minutes. Stir in 1 teaspoon salt and ½ teaspoon black pepper.

Chili con Carne

HOMEMADE AND SIMPLE—EVERYONE LOVES
CHILI. REHEATING JUST MAKES IT BETTER.

SIDE: Green Chile and Cheese Corn
Bread (page 164).

DESSERT: Cookies and ice cream.

MAKES: 8 servings

1½	pounds ground beef
2	cups finely chopped onion
1	cup finely chopped green bell pepper
1	tablespoon minced fresh garlic
2	tablespoons chili powder (or to taste)
2	teaspoons ground cumin
1	teaspoon dried oregano, crushed
1	teaspoon salt
¼	teaspoon cayenne pepper (or to taste)
2	cups water
1	15-ounce can diced tomatoes, undrained
¼	cup tomato paste
1	teaspoon sugar
	Shredded cheddar cheese
	Onion, finely chopped
	Sour cream

ONE In a 4- to 6-quart Dutch oven or large chili pot over medium-high heat cook ground beef, onion, bell pepper, and garlic until beef is brown. Drain off fat. Stir in chili powder, cumin, oregano, salt, and cayenne pepper; cook 1 minute. Stir in water, undrained tomatoes, tomato paste, and sugar.

TWO Bring to boiling. Turn heat to low. Simmer, uncovered, for 25 to 30 minutes, stirring occasionally. Top chili with cheese, onion, and sour cream.

FREEZE AHEAD: Place cooked chili in a freezer bag and freeze up to 2 months. Defrost completely in refrigerator. Reheat over medium heat until hot and bubbly.

Swedish Meatballs

SOUR CREAM MAKES THIS SAUCE RICH AND CREAMY.

SIDES: Buttered noodles and Red Raspberry Ring (page 187).

DESSERT: Easy Apple Crisp (page 233).

MAKES: 6 to 8 servings

- 2 cups canned beef broth
- ¼ cup water
- 2 tablespoons all-purpose flour
- ½ teaspoon paprika
- ½ cup sour cream
- ½ cup sliced green onion
- 1 teaspoon salt
- ½ teaspoon black pepper
- ½ teaspoon Kitchen Bouquet®
- 1 recipe Basic Meatballs (page 35), cooked

ONE For sauce, in a 4- to 6-quart Dutch oven or large saucepan bring beef broth to boiling over high heat.

TWO Meanwhile, in a small bowl whisk together water, flour, and paprika until smooth. While whisking the boiling broth, slowly add the flour mixture. Turn heat to medium-low. Let sauce simmer, whisking constantly, for 3 to 5 minutes or until thickened slightly.

THREE Stir sour cream, green onion, salt, pepper, and Kitchen Bouquet® into sauce. Carefully fold in cooked Basic Meatballs; heat through.

FREEZE AHEAD: Cook a double batch of Basic Meatballs. Place half the cooked meatballs in a freezer bag and freeze up to 2 months. Defrost completely in refrigerator.

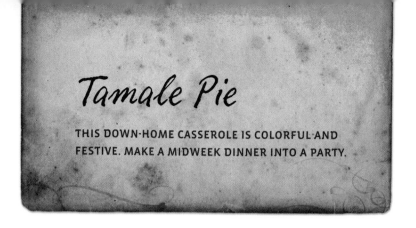

Tamale Pie

THIS DOWN-HOME CASSEROLE IS COLORFUL·AND FESTIVE. MAKE A MIDWEEK DINNER INTO A PARTY.

SIDE: Blue Cheese Wedge Salad (page 200).

DESSERT: Fishbowl Trifle (page 248)

MAKES: 6 servings

Nonstick cooking spray

- 1 pound ground beef
- ½ cup chopped onion
- ¾ cup chopped bell pepper
- 1 16-ounce can tomato sauce
- 1½ cups frozen corn
- ½ cup sliced, pitted black olives
- 1 tablespoon sugar
- 2 teaspoons chili powder
- 1 teaspoon minced fresh garlic
- 1 teaspoon salt
- 2 cups cold water
- ¾ cup cornmeal
- 1 tablespoon butter
- ½ teaspoon salt

ONE Preheat oven to 375°F. Coat a 13×9×2-inch baking dish with cooking spray.

TWO In a large skillet cook ground beef, onion, and bell pepper over medium heat until meat is brown. Drain off fat. Stir in tomato sauce, corn, olives, sugar, chili powder, garlic, and 1 teaspoon of the salt. Simmer 20 minutes. Transfer to prepared baking dish.

THREE In a saucepan stir together water, cornmeal, butter, and the remaining ½ teaspoon salt. Cook over medium heat, stirring constantly, until mixture thickens. (If mixture becomes too thick, add more water.) Spread cornmeal mixture evenly over meat mixture in baking dish.

FOUR Bake, uncovered, about 40 minutes or until corn bread crust is done in the center.

PLAN AHEAD: Prepare through Step Two, cover and refrigerate up to 2 days ahead. Preheat oven. Uncover and continue according to Step Three.

FREEZE AHEAD: Prepare through Step Three. Cover with plastic wrap and foil. Freeze up to 2 months. Defrost completely in refrigerator. Preheat oven. Remove plastic wrap and foil and continue according to Step Four.

Italian Meatball Hoagies

SOME NIGHTS YOU JUST NEED A BIG, MELTY, COMFORT SANDWICH. THIS ONE IS A BEAUTY.

SIDE: Sesame Broccoli (page 207).

DESSERT: Strawberry or peach ice cream with coconut macaroon cookies.

MAKES: 6 servings

- 1 recipe Basic Marinara Sauce (page 38)
- 1 recipe Basic Meatballs (page 35), cooked
- 6 hoagie buns, split
- 6 1-ounce slices provolone cheese

ONE In a large saucepan bring Basic Marinara Sauce to simmering over medium heat. Turn heat to low. Simmer 20 minutes. Carefully fold cooked Basic Meatballs into sauce; heat through.

TWO Preheat broiler. Place hoagie bun halves flat on a large baking sheet. Toast lightly; add meatballs and marinara to bottom half of bun. Top with cheese, return to broiler and broil until cheese is melted.

PLAN AHEAD: Prepare Basic Marinara Sauce and cooked Basic Meatballs up to 2 days ahead. Cover and refrigetate. Continue according to Step One.

FREEZE AHEAD: Place Basic Marinara Sauce and cooked Basic Meatballs in a freezer bag and freeze up to 2 months. Defrost completely in refrigerator. Continue according to Step One.

Hearty Beef and Penne Pasta

THIS CLASSIC BEEF AND PASTA DISH IS SATISFYING AND COMFORTING. LET YOUR KIDS HELP LAYER THE INGREDIENTS.

SIDES: Apricot-Glazed Carrots (page 212) and Parmesan Toast (page 163).

DESSERT: Vanilla pudding with strawberry sauce.

MAKES: 10 servings

Nonstick cooking spray

- 2 cups dried penne pasta
- 1 pound ground beef
- 1 recipe Basic Marinara Sauce (page 38)
- ½ cup canned sliced mushrooms
- ½ cup chopped onion
- 1 cup shredded mozzarella cheese

ONE Preheat oven to 375°F. Coat a 13×9×2-inch baking dish with cooking spray.

TWO Cook pasta according to package directions; drain and set aside.

THREE Meanwhile, in a large skillet cook ground beef until brown; drain off fat.

FOUR Spread ½ cup of the Basic Marinara Sauce in the bottom of the prepared baking dish. Top with cooked pasta, cooked ground beef, mushrooms, and onion. Pour remaining Basic Marinara Sauce evenly over all. Sprinkle with cheese.

FIVE Bake, uncovered, 30 to 40 minutes or until hot and bubbly.

PLAN AHEAD: Prepare through Step Four up to 2 days ahead. Cover and refrigerate. Preheat oven. Uncover and continue according to Step Five.

FREEZE AHEAD: Prepare through Step Four. Cover with plastic wrap and foil. Freeze up to 2 months. Defrost completely in refrigerator. Preheat oven. Remove plastic wrap and foil and continue according to Step Five.

pork

Apricot-Glazed Ham

MUSTARD AND APRICOT PRESERVES COMBINE TO MAKE THIS HAM HEAVENLY.

SIDE: Lemon Parmesan Risotto (page 155).

DESSERT: Chocolate Pecan Pie (page 240).

MAKES: 12 to 16 servings

1   10- to 12-pound cooked bone-in ham

   Whole cloves

½   cup apricot preserves

¼   cup Dijon mustard

1   cup packed brown sugar

2   cups apple juice

1   pound dried apricot halves

   Maple syrup

   Dijon mustard

ONE Preheat oven to 350°F. With a sharp knife, carefully cut off the thick rind and most of the excess fat from the top of the ham, being careful not to cut through to the meat. Score ham in a diamond pattern. Place ham in a shallow roasting pan. Stud ham with whole cloves at the point of each diamond.

TWO Melt apricot preserves in a small saucepan over low heat. Brush preserves over surface of ham. Spread the ¼ cup mustard over the preserves. Pat brown sugar on top of the mustard.

THREE Pour apple juice into roasting pan. Bake for 45 minutes, basting frequently. Add apricots to the roasting pan. Bake, uncovered, 45 minutes more or until ham is glazed and brown.

FOUR Remove ham from oven. Use toothpicks to secure an apricot half in each diamond pattern. Let stand 15 minutes before carving. Serve with maple syrup and additional mustard.

PLAN AHEAD: Prepare through Step One up to 3 days ahead. Cover and refrigerate. Continue according to Step Two.

FREEZE AHEAD: Prepare through Step Two. Wrap carefully with plastic wrap and foil. Freeze up to 2 months. Defrost completely in refrigerator. Preheat oven. Remove plastic wrap and foil and continue according to Step Three.

Ham and Corn Chowder

THICK AND RICH, THIS SOUP MAKES A HEARTY MEAL.

SIDE: Corn bread muffins.

DESSERT: Rice Pudding (page 249).

MAKES: 8 servings

- 2 or 3 slices bacon, slivered
- ½ cup chopped onion
- ½ cup chopped carrot
- ½ cup chopped celery
- ½ cup chopped roasted red bell pepper
- 2 cups milk
- 1 15-ounce jar Alfredo pasta sauce
- 2 cups frozen corn
- 2 cups canned creamed corn
- 1 cup diced cooked ham
- 1 4-ounce can diced green chile peppers, undrained
- 1 teaspoon dried oregano, crushed
- 1 teaspoon Worcestershire sauce
- 1 teaspoon salt
- ¼ teaspoon black pepper

ONE In a 4- to 6-quart Dutch oven or soup pot cook bacon over medium-high heat until crisp. Remove bacon with a slotted spoon; set aside. Add onion, carrot, celery, and roasted bell pepper to Dutch oven; cook and stir until vegetables are tender.

TWO Return cooked bacon to Dutch oven along with milk, pasta sauce, corn, creamed corn, ham, undrained chile peppers, oregano, Worcestershire sauce, salt, and black pepper.

THREE Bring chowder to simmering. Simmer gently, uncovered, for 25 to 30 minutes, stirring often to avoid scorching.

PLAN AHEAD: Prepare through Step Two up to 2 days ahead. Cover and refrigerate. Continue according to Step Three.

FREEZE AHEAD: Place cooked soup in a freezer bag and freeze up to 2 months. Defrost completely in refrigerator. Reheat over low heat.

Baked Potato Soup

COMBINE ALL THE FLAVORS OF A LOADED BAKER IN A CREAMY SOUP.

SIDES: Focaccia bread and Spinach Salad (page 196).

DESSERT: Caramel Fruit: Place sliced bananas, strawberries, or other fresh fruit in a dessert bowl; drizzle with caramel sauce.

MAKES: 6 to 8 servings

- 6 slices bacon, slivered
- 1 cup chopped onion
- ⅔ cup all-purpose flour
- 6 cups chicken broth
- 4 cups diced baked potato
- 2 cups milk
- ¼ cup chopped fresh parsley
- 2 teaspoons dried basil, crushed
- 2 teaspoons salt
- 1 teaspoon minced fresh garlic
- ½ teaspoon black pepper
- 1 cup shredded cheddar cheese
- ½ cup sliced green onion
  Bottled hot pepper sauce
  Crisp-cooked bacon (optional)
  Shredded cheddar cheese (optional)
  Sour cream (optional)
  Italian parsley (optional)

ONE In a 4- to 6-quart Dutch oven or soup pot over medium-high heat cook bacon and onion until bacon is crisp. Remove with a slotted spoon; set aside. Reserve 2 tablespoons of the drippings in the Dutch oven. Use a whisk to stir flour into reserved drippings. Cook for 2 to 3 minutes, whisking constantly. Gradually add chicken broth, whisking to prevent lumps. Cook and whisk until mixture thickens. Add potato, milk, parsley, basil, salt, garlic, and black pepper to Dutch oven. Simmer for 5 minutes, stirring often.

TWO Add the 1 cup cheese and the green onion to Dutch oven, stirring until cheese melts and soup is heated through. Season to taste with hot pepper sauce.

THREE If desired, top each serving with additional bacon, cheese, sour cream, and/or Italian parsley.

PLAN AHEAD: When serving baked potatoes at another meal, bake extra to use in this soup. Soup can be prepared up to 3 days ahead. Cover and refrigerate. Reheat over low heat.

FREEZE AHEAD: Place cooked soup in a freezer bag and freeze up to 2 months. Defrost completely in refrigerator. Reheat over low heat.

Gabriel's Eggs

MILD GREEN CHILES AND CHEDDAR CHEESE
MELD DELICIOUSLY IN THIS DISH. IT'S GREAT
FOR BREAKFAST, A LADIES' BRUNCH, OR A
COZY FAMILY SUPPER.

SIDES: Apple-Walnut-Raisin Spinach Salad (page 197) and Cheesy Biscuits (page 170).

DESSERT: Pudding Fruit Sundaes: Top prepared pudding with sliced strawberries, peaches, or other fresh fruit.

MAKES: 6 to 8 servings

- 1 pound bulk pork sausage
- 8 slices sourdough French bread
- 4 cups shredded cheddar cheese
- 6 eggs
- 3 cups milk
- 1 4-ounce can diced green chile peppers, undrained
- 1 teaspoon salt
- ¼ teaspoon black pepper

ONE In a skillet cook and crumble sausage until no longer pink; drain on paper towels.

TWO Arrange bread slices in the bottom of a 13×9×2-inch baking dish, tearing to fit if necessary. Sprinkle cooked sausage evenly over bread; top with cheese. Beat together eggs, milk, undrained chile peppers, salt, and black pepper; pour over cheese. Cover and refrigerate at least 1 hour or up to 2 days.

THREE Preheat oven to 325°F. Bake, uncovered, for 1½ hours.

PLAN AHEAD: Prepare through Step Two up to 2 days ahead. Cover and refrigerate. Preheat oven. Uncover and continue according to Step Three.

FREEZE AHEAD: Prepare through Step Two. Cover with plastic wrap and foil. Freeze up to 2 months. Defrost completely in refrigerator. Preheat oven. Remove plastic wrap and foil and continue according to Step Three.

Open-Face Bacon, Tomato, and Cheese Sandwiches

MY BIG SISTER BARBARA LEARNED TO MAKE THESE SANDWICHES IN HER HOME ECONOMICS CLASS WHEN I WAS A LITTLE GIRL. THIS WAS THE FIRST RECIPE I EVER LEARNED. I HAVE BEEN MAKING THESE EVER SINCE, AND IT IS STILL MY FAVORITE SANDWICH.

SIDE: Greek Potato Salad (page 184).

DESSERT: Hello Dolly Bars (page 229).

MAKES: 4 sandwiches

8	slices bacon
4	slices dense country-style bread
4	to 8 tablespoons mayonnaise
12	slices tomato
1	teaspoon salt (or to taste)
1	teaspoon black pepper (or to taste)
1½	cups shredded cheddar cheese

ONE In a skillet cook bacon until crisp; drain on paper towels.

TWO Preheat broiler. Arrange bread slices on a baking sheet. Spread each slice of bread with some of the mayonnaise. Top with bacon, breaking the slices to fit. Top with tomato slices; sprinkle with salt and pepper. Top with cheddar cheese. If desired, dollop with extra mayonnaise.

THREE Broil about 4 inches from the heat until cheese is hot and begins to bubble. Turn off broiler. Let sandwiches sit in closed oven for 5 minutes before serving.

PLAN AHEAD: When cooking bacon for another meal, prepare extra to use in these sandwiches.

Rosemary-Roasted Pork Loin

FRESH ROSEMARY IS THE SECRET TO THIS INCREDIBLE PORK LOIN. YOUR HOUSE WILL SMELL HEAVENLY WHEN YOU COOK THIS DISH.

SIDES: Asparagus Baked with Cheese (page 220) and Fruit and Nut Couscous (page 175).

DESSERT: Caramel Banana Pound Cake: Top slices of purchased pound cake with sliced bananas, caramel sauce, and thawed whipped dessert topping.

MAKES: 4 to 6 servings

Nonstick cooking spray

2 cloves garlic

1 2- to 2½-pound pork tenderloin

2 sprigs fresh rosemary, cut into 1-inch pieces

2 teaspoons salt

1 teaspoon black pepper

2 tablespoons olive oil

1 cup chicken broth or water

ONE Preheat oven to 375°F. Coat a 13×9×2-inch baking dish with cooking spray. Cut each garlic clove into 4 slices.

TWO Use a sharp knife to make 8 small slits in tenderloin. Push 1 slice of garlic and 1 piece of rosemary into each slit. Sprinkle tenderloin with salt and pepper.

THREE Preheat oil in a skillet over medium heat. Brown tenderloin on all sides. Transfer to prepared baking dish; pour broth into dish. Bake, covered, for 30 to 45 minutes or until desired doneness (145°F to 155°F).

FOUR Let stand for 10 minutes. If desired, drizzle with pan juices.

PLAN AHEAD: Prepare through Step Two up to 2 days ahead. Continue according to Step Three.

FREEZE AHEAD: Prepare through Step Two. Place in a freezer bag and freeze up to 2 months. Defrost completely in refrigerator. Continue according to Step Three.

Stuffed Pork Tenderloin

MY DAUGHTER LOVES TO MAKE THIS DISH BECAUSE OF ITS "HOLLYWOOD" PRESENTATION. NO ONE WILL EVER GUESS HOW EASY IT IS TO CREATE. THE DRESSING KEEPS THE MEAT MOIST FROM THE INSIDE, AND THE BACON DOES THE SAME ON THE OUTSIDE. THIS ONE IS ALWAYS A WINNER.

SIDE: Sweet Potatoes and Apples (page 218).

DESSERT: Apple coffee cake served with caramel swirl ice cream.

MAKES: 6 to 8 servings

Nonstick cooking spray

2 tablespoons butter

1 cup finely chopped onion

1 cup finely chopped celery

1 8-ounce package dry herb stuffing mix

2 pork tenderloins (each about ¾ pound)

8 slices bacon

ONE Preheat oven to 350°F. Coat a 13×9×2-inch baking dish with cooking spray.

TWO In a large skillet saute onion and celery in hot butter until tender. Prepare stuffing mix according to package directions, adding the cooked onion and celery.

THREE Butterfly each tenderloin by making a lengthwise cut in the meat. Spread open each tenderloin and flatten. Mound stuffing along the entire surface of one of the tenderloins. Lay the second tenderloin on top of the stuffing. Mold tenderloins into a cylinder.

FOUR Place stuffed meat in the prepared baking dish. Top with strips of bacon, tucking ends of bacon under meat. (Place any extra stuffing around meat.)

FIVE Bake, uncovered, about 1 hour or until internal temperature of stuffing is 160°F. Let stand 5 minutes.

PLAN AHEAD: Prepare through Step Four up to 1 day ahead. Cover and refrigerate. Preheat oven. Uncover and continue according to Step Five.

FREEZE AHEAD: Prepare through Step Four. Cover with plastic wrap and foil. Freeze up to 2 months. Defrost completely in refrigerator. Preheat oven. Remove plastic wrap and foil and continue according to Step Five.

Pork Loin Kabobs

PORK TENDERLOIN IS WONDERFUL BECAUSE THERE IS VIRTUALLY NO WASTE. USE THE VEGETABLES YOUR FAMILY LIKES TO CREATE KABOBS THEY WILL LOVE.

SIDE: Garlic-Roasted Potatoes (page 219).

DESSERT: Pineapple with Ice Cream: Drain canned pineapple slices. Place on a grill rack (or broiler pan) after kabobs are removed; grill (or broil) until warm. Top each slice with a scoop of vanilla ice cream.

MAKES: 6 servings

- 1 cup Balsamic Maple Vinaigrette (page 199)
- 1 tablespoon honey
- 1 teaspoon minced fresh garlic
- 1½ pounds pork tenderloin, cut into 1-inch cubes
- 2 medium zucchini, cut into 1-inch pieces
- 1 green bell pepper, cut into 1-inch pieces
- 1 red bell pepper, cut into 1-inch pieces
- 1 onion, cut into 1-inch pieces
- 6 12-inch metal skewers

ONE For marinade, in a bowl stir together Balsamic Maple Vinaigrette, honey, and garlic. Add pork cubes, zucchini, green bell pepper, red bell pepper, and onion. Cover and marinate in refrigerator for 2 hours.

TWO Drain pork and vegetables, reserving marinade. Alternately thread pork and vegetables onto skewers.

THREE Preheat grill to medium heat (or preheat broiler). Grill (or broil) skewers for 12 to 15 minutes or until meat is cooked through.

FOUR Meanwhile, transfer marinade to a small saucepan; boil for 2 to 3 minutes. Serve kabobs with marinade.

PLAN AHEAD: Cut up meat and vegetables 1 day ahead. Refrigerate in a resealable plastic bag.

FREEZE AHEAD: Prepare through Step Two. Place kabobs in a freezer container; cover with marinade. Freeze up to 2 months. Defrost completely in refrigerator. Drain kabobs, reserving marinade. Continue according to Step Three.

Sweet and Sour Pork

THIS SIMPLE RECIPE YIELDS AN IRRESISTIBLE SWEET AND SOUR COMBINATION.

SIDE: Fried Rice (page 157).

DESSERT: Lemon sorbet or sherbert.

MAKES: 6 servings

- 1 20-ounce can pineapple chunks
- ½ cup water
- ½ cup vinegar
- ½ cup packed brown sugar
- 2 tablespoons ketchup
- 2 tablespoons soy sauce
- 2 pounds boneless pork, cut into 1-inch cubes
- 1½ teaspoons salt
- ½ teaspoon garlic salt
- ½ teaspoon black pepper
- 2 tablespoons vegetable oil
- 2 tablespoons cornstarch
- 1 large bell pepper, cut into 1-inch pieces
- 1 large onion, cut into 1-inch pieces
- Hot cooked rice

ONE Drain pineapple, reserving juice in a bowl. Add water, vinegar, brown sugar, ketchup, and soy sauce to pineapple juice; set aside.

TWO Sprinkle pork cubes with salt, garlic salt, and black pepper. Preheat oil in a large skillet over medium-high heat. Brown pork cubes in hot oil. Turn heat to low. Add 1 cup of the pineapple juice mixture to skillet. Cover and simmer gently about 20 minutes or until pork is tender.

THREE Add cornstarch to the remaining pineapple juice mixture, whisking to break up any lumps; whisk into skillet. Turn heat to high, whisking constantly until mixture boils and thickens.

FOUR Add pineapple chunks, bell pepper, and onion to skillet. Cook about 5 minutes more or until vegetables are heated through. Serve over rice.

PLAN AHEAD: Prepare through Step Two up to 2 days ahead. Cover and refrigerate. Continue according to Step Three.

FREEZE AHEAD: Prepare through Step Three. Place in a freezer bag and freeze up to 2 months. Defrost completely in refrigerator. Continue according to Step Four.

Orange-Apricot-Glazed Pork Chops

OUR SUPER SUPPERS FAMILIES LOVE THESE CHOPS.
ADULTS LIKE THE SWEET AND SOUR COMBINATION
AND KIDS THINK IT'S DESSERT.

SIDE: Lemon-Butter Edamame
(page 211).

DESSERT: Apple pie drizzled with
caramel sauce.

MAKES: 6 servings

2 tablespoons canola oil

6 boneless pork top loin chops,
cut 1 inch thick

1 cup packed brown sugar

½ cup orange marmalade

½ cup apricot preserves

¼ cup Dijon mustard

ONE In a large skillet cook chops in hot oil over
medium-high heat about 14 minutes or until done
(160°F), turning once. Transfer chops to a serving
platter; keep warm.

TWO For sauce, add brown sugar, marmalade,
preserves, and mustard to skillet. Bring to boiling.
Pour sauce over chops.

FREEZE AHEAD: Prepare through Step Two.
Place in a freezer bag and freeze up to 2 months.
Defrost completely in refrigerator. Reheat over
low heat.

Pork Chops with Apple and Herb Dressing

THE CHOPS BAKE ON TOP OF THE DRESSING, ALLOWING ALL THE FLAVORS TO MINGLE.

SIDE: Buttered peas.

DESSERT: Chocolate pudding.

MAKES: 6 servings

Nonstick cooking spray

- 4 cups corn bread stuffing mix
- 2 cups canned apple slices, undrained
- 1½ cups finely chopped celery
- 1½ cups finely chopped onion
- 2 teaspoons dried sage, crushed
- ½ teaspoon black pepper
- 2 cups chicken broth
- ½ cup butter, melted
- 6 pork loin center-cut chops, cut 1 to 1¼ inches thick
- 1 tablespoon seasoned salt

ONE Preheat oven to 350°F. Coat a 13×9×2-inch baking dish with cooking spray.

TWO For dressing, stir together stuffing mix, undrained apple slices, celery, onion, sage, and pepper. Add broth and melted butter; toss to coat. Transfer dressing to the prepared baking dish; top with chops. Sprinkle chops with seasoned salt.

THREE Bake, covered, for 45 minutes. Uncover and bake 10 to 15 minutes more or until chops are done (160°F).

PLAN AHEAD: Prepare through Step Two up to 2 days ahead. Cover and refrigerate. Preheat oven. Uncover and continue according to Step Three.

FREEZE AHEAD: Prepare through Step Two. Cover with plastic wrap and foil. Freeze up to 2 months. Defrost completely in refrigerator. Preheat oven. Remove plastic wrap and foil and continue according to Step Three.

Pork Loin Chops with Sour Cherry Sauce

PORK AND FRUIT ARE A NATURAL COMBINATION. THE MARINATED CHERRY SAUCE IS DELICIOUS, SO BE SURE TO MAKE EXTRA TO SERVE OVER ICE CREAM.

SIDES: Buttered green beans and Tomato-Artichoke Heart Salad with Blue Cheese Dressing (page 183).

DESSERT: Lemon-Blueberry Tart: In the bottom of a 9-inch cookie-crumb piecrust spread one 16-ounce can blueberry pie filling. Prepare one 6-ounce package instant lemon pudding according to package directions; spread on top of pie filling. Refrigerate until ready to serve.

MAKES: 4 servings

- 1 cup dried sour cherries
- ½ cup port wine
- ½ cup prune juice
- 5 pork loin chops, cut 1 inch thick
- 1 teaspoon salt
- ¼ teaspoon black pepper
- 1 teaspoon butter
- 1 teaspoon olive oil
- ¼ cup balsamic vinegar

ONE In a small saucepan combine dried cherries, wine, and prune juice. Bring to simmering. Remove from heat. Let cherries stand while cooking chops.

TWO Season chops with salt and pepper. In a large skillet cook chops in hot butter and oil over medium-high heat about 14 minutes or until done (160°F), turning once. Transfer chops to a serving platter; keep warm. Remove skillet from heat.

THREE For sauce, add balsamic vinegar to skillet. Use a wooden spoon to scrape up any bits in the skillet. Return skillet to heat; add cherries and liquid. Simmer for 1 minute. Spoon sauce over chops.

FREEZE AHEAD: Prepare through Step Three, except transfer cooked pork chops to a 9×13×2-inch baking dish. Pour cherry sauce over chops. Cover with plastic wrap and foil. Freeze up to 2 months. Defrost completely in refrigerator. Preheat oven to 350°F. Remove plastic wrap and foil and bake about 20 minutes or until heated through.

Mom's Tender Pork Chops

THESE CHOPS ARE SIMPLE, AND THE BROWNED ONION SLICES ADD GREAT FLAVOR.

SIDE: Creamed Corn Casserole (page 203).

DESSERT: Strawberries and Cream Cake: Stir one 6-ounce package frozen strawberries, thawed, into 2 cups thawed whipped dessert topping. Spoon over four 1-inch slices purchased pound cake. Drizzle with chocolate sauce.

MAKES: 4 servings

- 4 sirloin pork chops (with or without the bone), cut ½ inch thick
- 2 teaspoons salt
- 1 teaspoon black pepper
- 2 tablespoons olive oil
- 1 large onion, cut into 4 thick slices
- 1 cup chicken broth or apple juice

ONE Sprinkle chops with salt and pepper. In a large skillet brown chops in hot oil, turning once. Remove chops from skillet. Add onion slices to skillet. Brown both sides of the onion slices, carefully turning with a wide spatula.

TWO Return chops to skillet, topping each with one onion slice. Pour broth over chops.

THREE Cover and simmer about 20 minutes or until chops are done (160°F). To serve, pour pan juices over onion-topped chops.

FREEZE AHEAD: Prepare through Step One. Place in a freezer bag and freeze up to 2 months. Defrost completely in refrigerator. Continue according to Step Two.

Kielbasa and Sauerkraut

THIS IS A GREAT DINNER TO KEEP ON THE STOVE ON GAME DAYS. IT CAN SIMMER SLOWLY FOR A LONG TIME AND JUST GETS BETTER AND BETTER. BE SURE TO SERVE WITH A GOOD DIJON MUSTARD FOR DIPPING THE SAUSAGE AND SPREADING ON THE SAUERKRAUT.

PORK

SIDES: Dijon mustard, rye bread, sliced onions, and Simple Tortellini Salad (page 192).

DESSERT: No-Bake Chocolate Cookies (page 227).

MAKES: 6 servings

- 1 pound cooked kielbasa or other cooked smoked sausage, cut into 2-inch pieces
- 4 cups water
- 1 28-ounce jar sauerkraut, undrained
- 8 new potatoes, cut into quarters
- 2 medium onions, thickly sliced

ONE In a 4- to 6-quart Dutch oven or soup pot combine sausage, water, undrained sauerkraut, potato, and onion. Bring to boiling.

TWO Turn heat to low. Cover and simmer 30 to 60 minutes or until potato is tender.

PLAN AHEAD: Prepare through Step Two up to 2 days ahead. Cover and refrigerate. Reheat over medium heat.

FREEZE AHEAD: Prepare through Step Two. Place in a freezer bag and freeze up to 2 months. Defrost completely in refrigerator. Reheat over medium heat.

Sausage and Cinnamon Apples

A COZY FALL DINNER IS SURE TO CREATE FUN MEMORIES AS KIDS DIP THEIR SAUSAGE INTO THE APPLE MIXTURE. THIS DISH ALWAYS HERALDED THE FALL SEASON AT OUR HOUSE.

SIDE: Stuffed Greek Bread (page 162).

DESSERT: Broiler S'Mores: Place graham crackers on a baking sheet. Top with chocolate and marshmallows; broil until marshmallows melt. Top with another graham cracker and serve.

MAKES: 6 servings

- 1   16-ounce tube ground seasoned sausage
- 2   16-ounce cans apple slices (not apple pie filling), undrained
- ½   cup packed brown sugar (or to taste)
- 1   teaspoon ground cinnamon
- 1   teaspoon butter
- ½   teaspoon vanilla

ONE Use a serrated knife to cut the sausage into ½-inch slices, cutting through the plastic tube; remove tube from around each slice. In a large skillet cook the sausage slices over medium-high heat until no pink remains.

TWO Meanwhile, place undrained apple slices in a saucepan. Add brown sugar and cinnamon to the apples. Bring to simmering over medium-low heat; stir in butter and vanilla.

THREE Serve the apple mixture over the cooked sausage slices.

PLAN AHEAD: Keep a tube of sausage in your refrigerator or freezer. A frozen tube will defrost in one day in your refrigerator. Canned apple slices can be kept in the pantry for quick cinnamon apples.

Sausage and Peppers with Rice

I LOVE THE FLAVOR OF BARBECUE SAUCE MIXED WITH SLICED SMOKED SAUSAGE. THESE ZESTY FLAVORS ARE PERFECT OVER THE MILD RICE.

SIDE: Sweet and Sour Coleslaw (page 179).

DESSERT: Cream Cheese Cupcakes (page 244).

MAKES: 8 servings

- 2 cups uncooked long grain white rice
- 2 tablespoons vegetable oil
- 1½ pounds cooked smoked sausage (such as kielbasa), cut into ½-inch pieces
- 2 cups thinly sliced bell pepper
- 2 cups thinly sliced onion
- 2 cups smoky barbecue sauce
- 1 15-ounce can diced tomatoes, undrained
- ½ cup water

ONE Prepare rice according to package directions.

TWO Preheat oil in a 4- to 6-quart Dutch oven or large soup pot over medium-high heat. Saute sausage pieces, bell pepper, and onion in hot oil until sausage is brown and vegetables are tender. Stir in barbecue sauce, undrained tomatoes, and water. Turn heat to low. Simmer, uncovered, for 20 minutes.

THREE Place cooked rice on a large serving platter; top with sausage mixture.

PLAN AHEAD: Prepare through Step Two up to 2 days ahead. Cover and refrigerate sausage mixture. Place cooked rice in a resealable plastic bag and refrigerate. Reheat sausage mixture over low heat. To reheat rice, place bag in a microwave oven and heat on 100% power (high) about 1 minute or until rice is hot.

FREEZE AHEAD: Prepare through Step Two only. Place in a freezer bag and freeze up to 2 months. Defrost completely in refrigerator. Reheat over low heat while cooking rice.

SIDE: Beer Bread (page 172).

DESSERT: Chocolate Frosting Sundaes: Heat a container of prepared chocolate frosting in a microwave oven on 100% power (high) about 15 seconds or until melted. Drizzle melted frosting over scoops of ice cream.

Jambalaya

THIS RECIPE IS STREAMLINED TO MAKE IT EASY ON BUSY DAYS.

MAKES: 6 servings

- 2 tablespoons vegetable oil
- ½ pound andouille or other smoked sausage, chopped
- 1½ cups chopped onion
- 1 cup chopped celery
- ¾ cup chopped green bell pepper
- ⅔ cup chopped cooked ham
- 4 to 5 cloves garlic, minced
- 1½ pounds chicken, cut into bite-size pieces
- 4 medium tomatoes (about 1 pound), chopped
- 2 cups seafood or chicken broth
- 1 cup tomato sauce
- 1½ teaspoons salt
- ¾ teaspoon bottled hot pepper sauce
- 1 teaspoon black pepper
- 2 bay leaves
- ½ cup chopped green onion
  Creole seasoning
- 2 cups uncooked long grain white rice
- 18 medium peeled and deveined uncooked shrimp

ONE Preheat oil in a 4- to 6-quart Dutch oven over medium heat. Add sausage, onion, celery, bell pepper, ham, and garlic to Dutch oven. Saute for 5 to 6 minutes or until onions are tender.

TWO Add chicken; cook and stir for 1 minute. Add tomato, broth, tomato sauce, salt, hot pepper sauce, black pepper, and bay leaves. Cook for 15 minutes, stirring often. Stir in green onion; cook 2 minutes more. Season to taste with Creole seasoning.

THREE Preheat oven to 350°F. Remove Dutch oven from heat. Stir in uncooked rice and shrimp. Bake, covered, about 20 minutes or until rice is tender and shrimp are opaque, stirring halfway through baking. Remove bay leaves before serving.

PLAN AHEAD: Prepare through Step Two up to 2 days ahead. Cover and refrigerate. Continue according to Step Three.

FREEZE AHEAD: Prepare through Step Three. Place in a freezer container and freeze up to 2 months. Defrost completely in refrigerator. To reheat, preheat oven to 350°F. Transfer to a baking dish and bake about 30 minutes or until heated through.

Pasta Pie with Kielbasa

PARMESAN CHEESE IN THE PASTA CRUST MAKES THE CRUST GOOD ENOUGH TO EAT BY ITSELF. USE OTHER MEATS, IF DESIRED, SUCH AS CHOPPED COOKED CHICKEN OR TURKEY, SLICED PEPPERONI, OR COOKED GROUND BEEF.

SIDE: Caesar Salad (page 193).

DESSERT: Lemon Curd Sundaes: Top scoops of ice cream with purchased lemon curd.

MAKES: 6 servings

Nonstick cooking spray

- 6 ounces dried macaroni or spaghetti
- 2 eggs, slightly beaten
- ½ cup shredded Parmesan cheese
- 1 tablespoon olive oil
- 4 ounces cooked kielbasa, thinly sliced
- 2 tomatoes, thinly sliced
- 1 teaspoon salt
- ½ teaspoon black pepper
- 2 cups shredded cheddar cheese

ONE Preheat oven to 375°F. Coat a 9-inch pie plate with cooking spray.

TWO Cook pasta according to package directions; drain. Stir eggs, Parmesan cheese, and oil into cooked pasta. Press pasta mixture onto bottom and up sides of prepared pie plate to form a crust.

THREE Top pasta crust with kielbasa and tomatoes. Sprinkle with salt and pepper. Top with cheese.

FOUR Bake about 20 minutes or until heated through.

PLAN AHEAD: Prepare through Step Three up to 2 days ahead. Cover and refrigerate. Preheat oven. Uncover and continue according to Step Four.

FREEZE AHEAD: Prepare through Step Three. Cover with plastic wrap and foil. Freeze up to 2 months. Defrost completely in refrigerator. Preheat oven. Remove plastic wrap and foil and continue according to Step Four.

poultry

SIDE: Spinach Salad (page 196).

DESSERT: Instant Fruit Tarts: Fill prepared individual tart shells with instant vanilla pudding; top with fresh fruit. Melt apple jelly; brush over fruit. Refrigerate until serving time.

Sausage, Chicken, and White Bean Cassoulet

TRADITIONAL FRENCH CASSOULET CONTAINS PRESERVED GOOSE OR DUCK, BUT CHICKEN WORKS JUST FINE.

MAKES: 10 servings

4 slices bacon, slivered

2 cups coarsely chopped onion

½ cup sliced celery

¼ cup chopped bell pepper

2 cloves garlic, minced

4 links sweet Italian sausage, pricked with a fork

1 3- to 3½-pound chicken, cut into 8 pieces

2 15-ounce cans cannellini beans, undrained

1 28-ounce can chopped or diced tomatoes, undrained

½ cup dry white wine

1 tablespoon Worcestershire sauce

1 tablespoon Creole seasoning

2 teaspoons herbes de Provence

½ teaspoon salt (or to taste)

¼ teaspoon black pepper

1 recipe Croutons (page 166)

Grated Parmesan cheese

ONE In a 4- to 6-quart Dutch oven cook bacon over medium-high heat until crisp. Remove bacon with a slotted spoon; set aside. Add onion, celery, bell pepper, and garlic to drippings in Dutch oven. Cook and stir until tender. Remove vegetables from Dutch oven; set aside.

TWO Add sausage links to the remaining drippings in the Dutch oven. Cook until brown, turning frequently. Remove from Dutch oven; cut into 1-inch pieces.

THREE Cook chicken, a few pieces at a time, in Dutch oven until golden brown.

FOUR Return all chicken to Dutch oven along with the cooked bacon, cooked vegetables, and sliced sausages. Add the undrained beans, undrained tomatoes, wine, Worcestershire sauce, Creole seasoning, and herbes de Provence. Turn heat to medium-low. Cover and simmer gently for 1 hour. Stir in salt and black pepper.

FIVE To serve, top each serving with croutons and sprinkle with Parmesan cheese.

Chicken Cacciatore

CACCIATORE IS ITALIAN FOR "HUNTER," AND THIS DISH WAS TRADITIONALLY PREPARED WITH WHATEVER MEAT CAME FROM THE DAY'S HUNT.

SIDES: Bruschetta (page 168) and tossed green salad.

DESSERT: Cheesecake served with sliced fresh strawberries.

MAKES: 4 servings

- 1   3- to 3½-pound chicken, cut into 8 pieces, or 4 chicken breast halves
- 1   tablespoon salt
- 2   tablespoons vegetable oil
- 1   large onion, sliced and separated into rings
- 8   ounces fresh mushrooms, sliced
- 1   teaspoon minced fresh garlic
- 1   cup dry white wine
- 1   28-ounce can chopped tomatoes, undrained
- 1   8-ounce can tomato sauce
- ½   cup pitted kalamata olives
- 2   tablespoons capers
- 1   tablespoon dried Italian mixed herbs, crushed

     Hot cooked spaghetti (optional)

ONE Sprinkle chicken pieces with salt. In a 12-inch skillet or 4- to 6-quart Dutch oven cook chicken pieces in hot oil, a few at a time, until golden brown. Remove chicken from skillet, reserving drippings in skillet. Add onion rings and mushrooms to skillet. Cook and stir for 2 to 3 minutes. Add garlic. Cook and stir 1 minute more. Add wine; cook for 3 to 5 minutes or until wine is reduced by half. Return chicken to skillet along with undrained tomatoes, tomato sauce, olives, capers, and Italian herbs.

TWO Cover and simmer gently about 35 minutes or until chicken is no longer pink. If desired, serve over spaghetti.

PLAN AHEAD: Prepare 1 day ahead. Cover and refrigerate. Reheat over low heat.

FREEZE AHEAD: Prepare through Step One. Place in a freezer bag and freeze up to 2 months. Defrost completely in refrigerator. Continue according to Step Two.

Parsley, Sage, Rosemary, and Thyme Chicken

SHOW OFF THIS BEAUTY BY CARVING IT AT THE TABLE.

SIDES: Garlic-Roasted Potatoes (page 219) and mixed vegetables.

DESSERT: Newlywed Peach Cobbler (page 236).

MAKES: 6 to 8 servings

- 1   5- to 7-pound Sunday roaster chicken
- ¼   cup butter, softened
- ¼   cup grated Parmesan cheese
- 1   tablespoon chopped fresh parsley
- 1   tablespoon chopped fresh sage
- 1   tablespoon chopped fresh rosemary
- 1   tablespoon chopped fresh thyme
- 2   teaspoons minced fresh garlic
- 1   teaspoon salt
- ¼   teaspoon black pepper
- 1   tablespoon olive oil
- 1   teaspoon seasoned salt

ONE Preheat oven to 375°F. Rinse inside of chicken; pat dry with paper towels. Use your fingers to lift the skin gently from the meat around the breast. Keep working your fingers under the skin around to each thigh and leg, lifting the skin as much as possible.

TWO Combine butter, Parmesan cheese, parsley, sage, rosemary, thyme, garlic, salt, and pepper. Use your fingers to spread the butter mixture evenly under the skin, making sure you spread it to the legs.

THREE Place chicken in a baking dish. If desired, tie the legs together with kitchen string. (The chicken will roast more evenly without this step.) Drizzle oil over chicken; sprinkle with seasoned salt.

FOUR Bake, uncovered, about 1¼ hours or until internal temperature reads 155°F. Cover chicken; let stand for 10 minutes before carving.

PLAN AHEAD: Prepare through Step Two up to 1 day ahead. Cover and refrigerate. Preheat oven. Uncover nd continue according to Step Three.

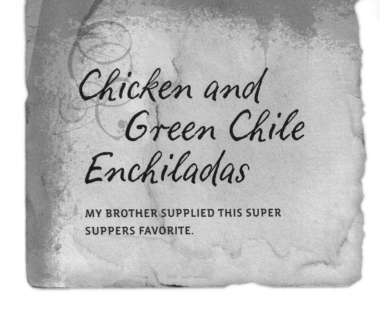

Chicken and Green Chile Enchiladas

MY BROTHER SUPPLIED THIS SUPER SUPPERS FAVORITE.

SIDES: Chef Duane's Spanish Rice (page 158) and sliced fresh fruit.

DESSERT: Drizzled Sugar Cookies: Arrange purchased sugar cookies on a piece of waxed paper. Heat a container of prepared chocolate frosting in a microwave oven on 100% power (high) for about 15 seconds or until melted; drizzle melted frosting over cookies.

MAKES: 10 servings

Nonstick cooking spray

- 1 **3-pound chicken, stewed and meat removed, or 3 boneless, skinless chicken breast halves (18 ounces total), poached (see pages 7-8) and chopped (about 3 cups)**
- 4 **cups shredded cheddar cheese**
- 10 **green onions, thinly sliced**
- 2 **teaspoons chili powder**
- 2 **10¾-ounce cans condensed cream of chicken soup**
- 2 **cups sour cream**
- 1 **7-ounce can diced green chile peppers, undrained**
- 12 **6-inch corn tortillas**

ONE Preheat oven to 350°F. Coat a 13×9×2-inch baking dish with cooking spray.

TWO In a large bowl stir together chopped chicken, 2 cups of the cheese, green onion, and chili powder. In another bowl combine soup, sour cream, and undrained chile peppers. Stir 1 cup of the soup mixture into the chicken mixture. Spread ½ cup of the soup mixture in the bottom of the prepared baking dish.

THREE Place ½ cup of the chicken mixture on 1 tortilla. Roll up tortilla; place in baking dish. Repeat with the remaining chicken mixture and tortillas. Place any remaining chicken mixture on top of rolled tortillas. Pour remaining soup mixture over tortillas; sprinkle with the remaining 2 cups cheese.

FOUR Bake, uncovered, for 35 to 45 minutes or until hot and bubbly.

PLAN AHEAD: Stew or poach chicken up to 2 days ahead. Cut up chicken and refrigerate in a resealable plastic bag.

FREEZE AHEAD: Prepare through Step Three. Cover with plastic wrap and foil. Freeze up to 2 months. Defrost completely in refrigerator. Preheat oven. Remove plastic wrap and foil and continue according to Step Four.

Chicken in a Bag

THIS RECIPE IS SO EASY, YOU CAN PUT IT ALL TOGETHER AFTER DINNER ONE NIGHT AND IT'S READY TO BAKE WHEN YOU GET HOME FROM WORK THE NEXT DAY.

SIDES: Mixed Field Greens with Candied Pecans and Goat Cheese (page 199) and sliced sourdough bread.

DESSERT: Angel food cake topped with ice cream and sliced fruit.

MAKES: 6 to 8 servings

- 1 5- to 7-pound Sunday roaster chicken
- 2 tablespoons vegetable oil
- 2 teaspoons salt
- 1 teaspoon dried thyme, crushed
- ½ teaspoon black pepper
- 1 large oven cooking bag
- 1 16-ounce package peeled fresh baby carrots
- 1 pound new potatoes
- 1 12-ounce package celery sticks
- 1 large onion, sliced
- ½ cup water

ONE Preheat oven to 350°F.

TWO RINSE Rinse cavity of chicken; pat dry with paper towels. Rub outside of chicken with oil; sprinkle with salt, thyme, and pepper.

THREE Prepare cooking bag according to manufacturer's directions. Place chicken in bag and surround with carrots, potatoes, celery, and onion; add water. Close bag according to manufacturer's directions.

FOUR Place cooking bag with chicken and vegetables on a large baking sheet. Bake for 1½ hours or until chicken is no longer pink. Carefully open bag. Let chicken stand for 10 minutes. Arrange chicken and vegetables on a serving platter; pour cooking juices over the top.

PLAN AHEAD: Leave cooked chicken and vegetables in the cooking bag; refrigerate up to 2 days. Preheat oven and reheat for 30 to 40 minutes.

FREEZE AHEAD: Prepare through Step Three. Place in a large freezer bag and freeze up to 2 months. Defrost completely in refrigerator. Preheat oven. Remove from freezer bag and continue according to Step Four.

Amish Chicken and Rice

I HAVE NO IDEA WHY THIS IS CALLED AMISH, ESPECIALLY SINCE IT CONTAINS WINE. IT'S AN OLD STANDBY, AND EVERY COOK NEEDS TO KNOW ABOUT IT. ALL INGREDIENTS CAN BE KEPT ON HAND. THE CHICKEN DOESN'T EVEN NEED TO BE THAWED. IF FROZEN, ADD A FEW MINUTES TO THE BAKING TIME.

SIDES: Buttered peas and fresh fruit salad.

DESSERT: My Mom's Strawberry Cake (page 242).

MAKES: 4 servings

Nonstick cooking spray

1½ cups uncooked long grain white rice

1 10¾-ounce can condensed cream of mushroom soup

1 10¾-ounce can condensed cream of celery soup

1 cup chicken broth

4 chicken breast halves

1 cup dry white wine

1 envelope dry onion soup mix

ONE Preheat oven to 350°F. Coat a 13×9×2-inch baking dish with cooking spray.

TWO In a bowl stir together uncooked rice, mushroom soup, celery soup, and chicken broth. Transfer to prepared baking dish. Arrange chicken breasts on top of rice mixture; pour wine over all. Sprinkle evenly with the soup mix.

THREE Bake, covered, about 1½ hours or until chicken is no longer pink.

FREEZE AHEAD: Prepare through Step Two. Cover with plastic wrap and foil. Freeze up to 2 months. Thaw completely in refrigerator. Preheat oven. Remove plastic wrap and foil and continue according to Step Three.

Chicken Dijon

THE CREAMY RANCH DRESSING AND TANGY MUSTARD ADD GREAT FLAVOR TO PLAIN CHICKEN BREASTS.

SIDE: Potatoes Cordon Bleu (page 206).

DESSERT: Sliced fresh peaches topped with vanilla yogurt.

MAKES: 6 servings

Nonstick cooking spray

- ½ cup bottled ranch salad dressing
- ½ cup Dijon mustard
- 1 cup Italian-seasoned bread crumbs
- 6 medium boneless, skinless chicken breast halves (2¼ pounds total)

ONE Preheat oven to 350°F. Coat a 13×9×2-inch baking dish with cooking spray.

TWO Stir together salad dressing and mustard. Put bread crumbs in a shallow dish. Use a pastry brush to coat both sides of each chicken breast half with the salad dressing mixture. Coat chicken with bread crumbs. Arrange chicken in the prepared baking dish.

THREE Bake, uncovered, about 20 minutes or until chicken is no longer pink.

FREEZE AHEAD: Prepare through Step Two. Cover with plastic wrap and foil. Freeze up to 1 month. Defrost completely in refrigerator. Preheat oven. Remove plastic wrap and foil and continue according to Step Three.

Maple-Mustard Chicken

THIS SUPER SUPPERS FAVORITE IS ALMOST GOOD ENOUGH FOR DESSERT.

SIDE: Lemon Parmesan Risotto (page 155).

DESSERT: Brownies crumbled and layered in a parfait glass with strawberries and whipped topping.

MAKES: 4 servings

- 2 tablespoons Dijon mustard
- 2 tablespoons maple syrup
- 2 tablespoons honey
- 2 teaspoons freshly squeezed lemon juice
- 1 3- to 3½-pound chicken, cut into 8 pieces
- 2 tablespoons vegetable oil

ONE In a large glass or stainless-steel bowl stir together the mustard, maple syrup, honey, and lemon juice. Add chicken pieces, turning to coat. Cover and refrigerate for 1 to 6 hours.

TWO Drain chicken, reserving mustard mixture. Preheat oil in a large skillet over medium-high heat. Brown chicken pieces on both sides. Turn heat to low. Pour mustard mixture over chicken. Cover and simmer gently for 30 to 40 minutes or until chicken is no longer pink.

THREE To serve, place chicken pieces on a large serving platter. Pour pan juices over chicken.

PLAN AHEAD: Prepare up to 2 days ahead. Cover and refrigerate. Reheat over low heat.

FREEZE AHEAD: Place chicken pieces and mustard mixture in a freezer bag and freeze up to 2 months. Defrost completely in refrigerator. Continue according to Step Two.

Parmesan Chicken

BUY CUT-UP CHICKENS TO MAKE THIS EASY
DISH EVEN FASTER.

SIDE: Fresh Cranberry-Orange Compote, chilled (page 221).

DESSERT: Pumpkin bars.

MAKES: 8 servings

Nonstick cooking spray

2   3- to 3½-pound chickens, each cut into 8 pieces, or 8 chicken breast halves

½   cup vegetable oil

1   cup grated Parmesan cheese

1   cup panko bread crumbs

1   teaspoon seasoned salt

½   teaspoon paprika

½   teaspoon garlic salt

ONE Preheat oven to 375°F. Coat a large baking sheet with cooking spray.

TWO Use a pastry brush to coat chicken pieces with oil. In a shallow dish combine Parmesan cheese, bread crumbs, seasoned salt, paprika, and garlic salt. Coat chicken with bread crumb mixture.

THREE Arrange chicken pieces on prepared baking sheet. Bake, uncovered, for 55 to 60 minutes or until no longer pink.

PLAN AHEAD: Cut up the chickens 1 day ahead. Cover and refrigerate.

FREEZE AHEAD: Prepare through Step Two. Place in a freezer container and freeze up to 2 months. Defrost completely in refrigerator. Preheat oven. Continue according to Step Three.

Sam's Fire Station Chicken

THIS RECIPE CAME FROM MY BROTHER, A RETIRED FIREFIGHTER AND A GREAT COOK. HE HAS SERVED MANY A BATCH OF THIS EASY, TASTY CHICKEN AT THE FIRE STATION AND AT HOME.

SIDE: Italian Green Beans and Potatoes (page 214).

DESSERT: Easy Apple Crisp (page 233).

MAKES: 4 servings

- 1 3- to 3½-pound chicken, cut into 8 pieces
- 1 28-ounce bottle smoky barbecue sauce
- 1 16-ounce can pineapple chunks, undrained
- 2 cups coarsely chopped onion
- 2 cups coarsely chopped bell pepper
- 1 teaspoon seeded and chopped fresh jalapeño chile pepper (or to taste) (optional)

ONE Place chicken pieces in a 4- to 6-quart Dutch oven. Add barbecue sauce, undrained pineapple chunks, onion, bell pepper, and, if desired, chile pepper to Dutch oven.

TWO Bring to boiling over medium-high heat. Turn heat to medium-low. Cover and simmer gently about 1 hour or until chicken is no longer pink.

FREEZE AHEAD: Place all ingredients in a freezer bag and freeze up to 2 months. Defrost completely in refrigerator. Continue according to Step Two.

Skillet Barbecue Chicken

YES, THERE ARE ONLY TWO INGREDIENTS.
I PULLED THIS TRICK MANY TIMES ON BUSY
SCHOOL DAYS, AND IT WAS ALWAYS A HIT.

SIDES: Cucumber-Onion Salad
(page 182) and buttered corn.

DESSERT: Cream Cheese Pie
(page 241).

MAKES: 4 servings

1 **3- to 3½-pound chicken,
cut into 8 pieces, or 4 chicken
breast halves**

3 **cups bottled smoky
barbecue sauce**

ONE Arrange chicken pieces in a large skillet. Pour
barbecue sauce over chicken.

TWO Cover and simmer over low heat for 30 to
40 minutes or until chicken is no longer pink.

FREEZE AHEAD: Place chicken pieces and barbecue
sauce in a freezer bag and freeze up to 2 months.
Defrost completely in refrigerator. Continue according
to Step Two.

Thai Chicken Wings

FISH SAUCE ADDS INCREDIBLE FLAVOR TO THIS SWEET AND SOUR SAUCE. THE ASIAN SAUCE SMELLS AWFUL THOUGH, SO YOU WILL HAVE TO TRUST ME ON THIS. MY DEAR FRIEND HELEN CHEN, DAUGHTER OF THE FAMOUS CHEF JOYCE CHEN, SAYS A BOTTLE OF FISH SAUCE WILL KEEP FOREVER IN THE PANTRY. SO GO AHEAD AND INVEST IN A BOTTLE AND MAKE LOTS OF THESE CHICKEN WINGS OVER THE YEARS.

SIDE: Sweet and Sour Coleslaw (page 179).

DESSERT: Frozen Adobe Pie (page 239).

MAKES: 4 to 6 servings

24	meaty chicken wings, tips removed, cut into wings and drumettes
8	cloves garlic, coarsely chopped
1	tablespoon grated fresh ginger
4	teaspoons soy sauce
4	teaspoons honey
2	teaspoons dried coriander, crushed
2	teaspoons fish sauce

ONE Place chicken wings in a large resealable plastic bag; add garlic, ginger, soy sauce, honey, coriander, and fish sauce. Seal bag; turn to coat chicken wings. Refrigerate for 2 to 24 hours.

TWO Preheat oven to 350°F.

THREE Place wings on a foil-lined baking sheet. Bake, uncovered, 15 minutes. Turn and bake 5 minutes more or until chicken is no longer pink. (Or broil 10 minutes. Turn and broil about 5 minutes more or until chicken is no longer pink.)

PLAN AHEAD: Prepare through Step One up to 24 hours ahead. Continue according to Step Two.

FREEZE AHEAD: Prepare through Step One and freeze up to 2 months. Defrost completely in refrigerator. Continue according to Step Two.

Chicken and White Bean Chili

ARE YOU CRUNCHED FOR TIME? PRECOOKED DELI CHICKEN COMES TO THE RESCUE.

SIDE: Green Chile and Cheese Corn Bread (page 164).

DESSERT: Chocolate chip cookies.

MAKES: 6 servings

- 1 purchased whole roasted chicken
- 2 tablespoons vegetable oil
- 1 cup chopped onion
- ½ cup chopped bell pepper
- 2 15-ounce cans white kidney beans, undrained
- 2 cups mild salsa
- 1 cup frozen corn
- 1 tablespoon chili powder
- 1 teaspoon ground cumin
- 2 tablespoons finely chopped fresh cilantro
- ½ teaspoon salt
- ¼ teaspoon black pepper
  Sour cream

ONE Remove meat from chicken, cutting into bite-size pieces; discard skin and bones. (You should have about 3 cups.) Set chicken aside.

TWO Preheat oil in a 6-quart Dutch oven or soup pot. Saute onion and bell pepper in hot oil until tender. Stir chopped chicken, undrained beans, salsa, corn, chili powder, and cumin into Dutch oven.

THREE Cover and simmer gently for 20 minutes. Just before serving, stir in cilantro, salt, and black pepper. Serve with sour cream.

PLAN AHEAD: Keep a roasted chicken in the freezer so you can be ready to make this recipe. Defrost chicken completely in refrigerator.

FREEZE AHEAD: Place cooked chili in a freezer bag and freeze up to 2 months. Defrost completely in refrigerator. Reheat over medium heat until hot and bubbly.

Chicken and Dumplings

MY MOM WAS A CHICKEN AND DUMPLINGS QUEEN. SHE MADE ALL VARIATIONS OF DUMPLINGS: ROLLED, DROPPED, AND EVEN POTATO GNOCCHI. SHE WOULD APPROVE OF TODAY'S COOKS USING CANNED BISCUITS BECAUSE THEY SAVE SO MUCH TIME, AND WITH FIVE KIDS, MY MOM WAS VERY PRACTICAL.

SIDES: Blue Cheese Wedge Salad (page 200) with sweet onions.

DESSERT: Baked Fruit (page 237).

MAKES: 8 servings

- 1 purchased whole roasted chicken
- 1 tablespoon vegetable oil
- 1 tablespoon butter
- 1½ cups sliced carrot
- 1½ cups sliced celery
- 1 cup chopped onion
- 4 cups water
- 2 14-ounce cans chicken broth
- 1 teaspoon dried thyme, crushed
- 1 bay leaf
- 1 12-ounce jar turkey gravy
- 1 teaspoon salt (or to taste)
- ¼ teaspoon black pepper (or to taste)
- 1 12-ounce can refrigerated buttermilk biscuits
- ¼ cup frozen peas

ONE Remove meat from chicken, cutting into bite-size pieces; discard skin and bones. (You should have about 3 cups.) Set chicken aside.

TWO Preheat oil and butter in a 6-quart Dutch oven or large soup pot over medium-high heat. Saute carrot, celery, and onion until tender. Stir in chopped chicken, water, chicken broth, thyme, and bay leaf. Turn heat to medium-low. Cover and simmer for 20 minutes. Remove bay leaf. Stir in gravy, salt, and pepper. Return to simmering.

THREE Cut each biscuit into 4 pieces. With chicken mixture simmering, drop in biscuits, a few at a time, pushing them down into the liquid with a wooden spoon. Cover and simmer 10 minutes. Carefully stir in peas; heat through.

PLAN AHEAD: Prepare through Step Two up to 2 days ahead. Cover and refrigerate. Reheat over low heat. Continue according to Step Three.

FREEZE AHEAD: Prepare through Step Two. Place chicken mixture in a freezer bag and freeze up to 2 months. Defrost completely in refrigerator. Reheat over medium heat until hot and bubbly. Continue according to Step Three.

Roasted Chicken Lasagna

PREPARED SPAGHETTI SAUCE MAKES THIS LASAGNA EASY TO PULL OFF.

SIDES: Garlic bread, tossed green salad, and Tomato-Basil Crostini (page 159).

DESSERT: Hello Dolly Bars (page 229).

MAKES: 12 servings

- 1 purchased whole roasted chicken

  Nonstick cooking spray
- 1 28-ounce jar spaghetti sauce
- 1 15-ounce can diced tomatoes, undrained
- 1 tablespoon chili powder
- 9 dried lasagna noodles
- 2 cups ricotta cheese or cottage cheese
- 1 teaspoon minced fresh garlic
- 1 egg, beaten
- 3 cups shredded mozzarella cheese

ONE Remove meat from chicken, cutting into bite-size pieces; discard skin and bones. (You should have about 3 cups.) Set chicken aside.

TWO Preheat oven to 350°F. Coat a 13×9×2-inch baking dish with cooking spray.

THREE For sauce, stir together spaghetti sauce, undrained tomatoes, and chili powder. Spread ½ cup of the sauce in the bottom of the prepared baking dish; top with 3 uncooked noodles. Cover with the chopped chicken. Pour 1 cup of the sauce over the chicken. Top with 3 more uncooked noodles. Cover noodles with 2 cups of the sauce.

FOUR Stir together ricotta cheese, garlic, and egg; dollop on top of sauce. Top with the remaining 3 uncooked noodles. Pour remaining sauce over all.

FIVE Bake, uncovered, about 45 minutes or until hot and bubbly. Sprinkle with mozzarella cheese; bake 10 minutes more.

PLAN AHEAD: Prepare through Step Four up to 2 days ahead. Cover and refrigerate. Preheat oven. Uncover and continue according to Step Five.

FREEZE AHEAD: Prepare through Step Four. Cover with plastic wrap and foil. Freeze up to 2 months. Defrost completely in refrigerator. Preheat oven. Remove plastic wrap and foil and continue according to Step Five.

Herbed Roasted Cornish Game Hens

GAME HENS ALWAYS MAKE DINNER SEEM ELEGANT AND SPECIAL. THEY ARE SO EASY TO BAKE, IT'S A SHAME TO SAVE THEM JUST FOR COMPANY.

POULTRY

SIDES: Curried Fruit (page 224) and warm dinner rolls and butter.

DESSERT: Peach ice cream and sugar cookies.

MAKES: 6 servings

Nonstick cooking spray

½ cup olive oil

2 teaspoons dried parsley flakes

2 teaspoons dried sage, crushed

2 teaspoons dried rosemary, crushed

2 teaspoons dried thyme, crushed

2 teaspoons minced fresh garlic

1 teaspoon salt

½ teaspoon black pepper

6 1½- to 2-pound Cornish game hens

2 heads fresh garlic, separated into cloves

1 large lemon, cut into 6 wedges

ONE Preheat oven to 375°F. Coat a large baking sheet with cooking spray.

TWO Stir together oil, parsley, sage, rosemary, thyme, garlic, salt, and pepper. Brush oil mixture evenly over each Cornish hen. Place Cornish hens on prepared baking sheet. Place several garlic cloves and a lemon wedge inside each hen.

THREE Bake, uncovered, about 1 hour or until internal temperature reads 165°F.

Chicken à la Provençal

CRISP, FRESH VEGETABLES MAKE THIS TRADITIONAL FRENCH
DISH HEALTHIER AND DELIGHTFUL.

SIDES: Buttered noodles and
Asparagus Baked with Cheese
(page 220).

DESSERT: Chocolate pound
cake layered with pudding in
a parfait glass.

MAKES: 4 servings

- 4 medium boneless, skinless chicken breast halves (1½ pounds total)
- 2 teaspoons salt
- ½ teaspoon black pepper
- ¼ cup olive oil
- 1 cup thinly sliced red bell pepper
- 1 cup thinly sliced yellow bell pepper
- 1 cup thinly sliced green bell pepper
- 1 cup thinly sliced onion
- 1 clove garlic, minced
- ¾ teaspoon dried basil, crushed
- ¾ teaspoon dried oregano, crushed
- 2 tablespoons balsamic vinegar

ONE Pound chicken breast halves flat with a rolling pin or use the palm of your hand to flatten breasts to an even thickness. Season both sides of each chicken breast half with 1 teaspoon of the salt and the black pepper.

TWO Preheat 2 tablespoons of the oil in a large skillet over medium-high heat. Add chicken to skillet. Cook for 3 to 5 minutes on each side or until no longer pink. Remove chicken from skillet; set aside.

THREE Add the remaining 2 tablespoons oil to the skillet along with the bell peppers and onion. Saute for 3 minutes. Add the remaining 1 teaspoon salt, garlic, basil, and oregano; saute for 1 minute more.

FOUR Return cooked chicken and any juices to the skillet; drizzle with vinegar. Bring to boiling. Turn heat to low. Cover and simmer about 5 minutes or until heated through.

PLAN AHEAD: Prepare vegetables up to 1 day ahead. Refrigerate in a resealable plastic bag.

Chicken Fried Rice

THIS FUN DISH IS A GREAT WAY TO GET KIDS TO
EAT VEGETABLES.

SIDES: Pita chips and egg drop soup.

DESSERT: Cinnamon Wontons:
Heat 1 inch of vegetable oil in a
deep skillet. Fry wonton wrappers
until golden brown. Drain on paper
towels; immediately sprinkle with
cinnamon and sugar. Serve warm
or at room temperature.

MAKES: 4 to 6 servings

- 2 tablespoons seasoned stir-fry
  oil or vegetable oil
- 2 cups small broccoli florets
- 1 cup chopped carrot
- 1 cup thinly sliced celery
- 1 cup chopped onion
- 1 small red bell pepper,
  thinly sliced
- 1 teaspoon minced fresh garlic
- 6 cups cooked rice
- 2 medium boneless, skinless
  chicken breast halves
  (12 ounces total), poached
  (see pages 7-8) and chopped
  (2 cups)
- 5 green onions, cut into
  1-inch pieces
- 1 8-ounce can sliced water
  chestnuts, drained
- ½ cup frozen peas
- ½ cup soy sauce

ONE Preheat oil in a wok or large nonstick skillet
over high heat. Add broccoli, carrot, celery, onion,
bell pepper, and garlic. Stir-fry for 2 minutes. Add
rice, chopped chicken, green onion, and water
chestnuts; stir-fry 1 minute. Add peas and soy sauce;
stir-fry 1 minute more.

PLAN AHEAD: Prepare vegetables and poach chicken
up to 1 day ahead. Refrigerate in a resealable
plastic bag.

Asian Chicken Noodle Salad

THESE NOODLES CAN BE HABIT-FORMING.

SIDE: Garlic breadsticks.

DESSERT: Miracle Pecan-Caramel Bars (page 226).

MAKES: 6 to 8 servings

- 12 ounces dried Chinese egg noodles or spaghetti
- 2 medium boneless, skinless chicken breast halves (12 ounces total), poached (see pages 7-8) and chopped (2 cups)
- 1 8-ounce can bamboo shoots, drained
- 1 8-ounce can water chestnuts, drained
- 1 cup canned baby corn
- 1 red bell pepper, thinly sliced
- 5 green onions, thinly sliced
- 1 cup mayonnaise
- 1 cup teriyaki sauce
- ¼ cup soy sauce
- 2 tablespoons toasted sesame oil
- 2 tablespoons freshly squeezed lemon juice
- 1 teaspoon salt (or to taste)

ONE Cook noodles according to package directions; drain.

TWO In a large bowl combine cooked noodles, chopped chicken, bamboo shoots, water chestnuts, baby corn, bell pepper, and green onion.

THREE For dressing, in a small bowl whisk together mayonnaise, teriyaki sauce, soy sauce, sesame oil, lemon juice, and salt. Pour dressing over chicken mixture; toss to coat.

PLAN AHEAD: Prepare up to 2 days ahead. Cover and refrigerate.

SIDES: Spinach with Lemon and Parmesan (page 215), garlic toast.

DESSERT: Black Forest Pudding: Top prepared chocolate pudding with cherry pie filling and a dollop of whipped dessert topping.

Mediterranean Chicken and Vegetables

OLIVES, GARLIC, AND FETA CHEESE COMBINE TO GIVE A BOLD, ROBUST FLAVOR.

MAKES: 6 servings

- 2 tablespoons olive oil
- 1 medium onion, cut into ½-inch slices
- 1 medium green bell pepper, cut into ½-inch slices
- 6 medium chicken breast halves, skinned (about 3 pounds)
- 1 28-ounce can diced tomatoes, undrained
- 1 15-ounce can garbanzo beans, drained
- 1 15-ounce can low-sodium chicken broth
- ¼ cup capers
- ¼ cup pitted kalamata olives
- ¼ cup roasted garlic cloves
- 2 tablespoons tomato paste
- 1 teaspoon dried oregano, crushed
- 1 bay leaf
- 1 teaspoon salt
- ½ teaspoon black pepper
- 1 zucchini, cut into ¼-inch slices
- 1 yellow summer squash, cut into ¼-inch slices
  Dried spaghetti or noodles
- ½ cup crumbled feta cheese

ONE In a large pot or 4- to 6-quart Dutch oven cook onion and bell pepper in hot oil until tender. Add chicken to Dutch oven. Stir together undrained tomatoes, garbanzo beans, chicken broth, capers, olives, garlic, tomato paste, oregano, bay leaf, salt, and black pepper; pour over chicken. Cover and simmer for 35 minutes. Remove bay leaf.

TWO Add zucchini and summer squash to Dutch oven. Cover and simmer about 15 minutes more or until internal temperature of the chicken reads 170°F.

THREE Meanwhile, cook pasta according to package directions; drain.

FOUR Serve chicken and vegetables over spaghetti. Sprinkle with crumbled feta cheese.

PLAN AHEAD: Prepare through Step Two up to 2 days ahead. Cover and refrigerate. Reheat over low heat. Continue according to Step Three.

FREEZE AHEAD: Prepare through Step Two. Place in a freezer bag and freeze up to 2 months. Defrost completely in refrigerator. Reheat over low heat. Continue according to Step Three.

Grilled Garlic Chicken with Mango Salsa

PERMEATED WITH GARLIC AND BASTED WITH PINEAPPLE JUICE, THIS CHICKEN IS SIMPLY BURSTING WITH FLAVOR.

SIDES: Guacamole and warm flour tortillas.

DESSERT: Instant Sopaipillas (page 231).

MAKES: 4 servings

- 8 cloves garlic
- 4 medium boneless, skinless chicken breast halves (1½ pounds total)
- 1 teaspoon salt
- ½ teaspoon black pepper
- ½ cup pineapple juice
- ¼ cup vegetable oil
- 1 recipe Mango Salsa (page 223)

ONE Preheat grill to medium heat. Cut each garlic clove into 2 to 4 slices.

TWO Use a sharp knife to make small slits in each chicken breast half. Push 1 garlic slice into each slit. Sprinkle chicken with salt and pepper. Stir together pineapple juice and oil; brush onto one side of each chicken breast half.

THREE Grill about 20 minutes or until chicken is no longer pink, brushing often with pineapple juice mixture and turning once halfway through grilling.

FOUR To serve, cut each chicken breast into ½-inch slices; top with Mango Salsa.

PLAN AHEAD: Prepare Mango Salsa up to 2 days ahead. Cover and refrigerate.

FREEZE AHEAD: Prepare through Step Three. Place in a freezer bag and freeze up to 2 months. Defrost completely in refrigerator. To reheat, place chicken in a baking dish and bake, covered, in a 350°F oven about 15 minutes or until heated through. Continue according to Step Four.

Lemon Chicken

ENJOY THIS BRIGHT AND CHEERFUL DISH— WITH LEMON AND CAPERS ADDING THE PERFECT ZING.

SIDE: Stir-Fried Bok Choy (page 205).

DESSERT: Fishbowl Trifle (page 248).

MAKES: 6 servings

- 6 boneless, skinless chicken breast halves (2¼ pounds total)
- 1 cup all-purpose flour
- 1 teaspoon lemon-pepper seasoning
- 1 teaspoon salt
- 2 tablespoons olive oil
- ¼ cup butter
- 2 tablespoons freshly squeezed lemon juice
- 1 tablespoon capers
- 1 tablespoon chopped fresh parsley

ONE Pound chicken breast halves flat with a rolling pin or use the palm of your hand to flatten breasts to an even thickness.

TWO Place flour, lemon-pepper seasoning, and salt in a plastic bag. Add chicken; shake bag to coat chicken.

THREE Preheat the oil and 2 tablespoons of the butter in a large skillet over medium-high heat. Add chicken to skillet. Cook, uncovered, for 3 to 5 minutes on each side or until no longer pink. Transfer chicken to a plate; keep warm.

FOUR For sauce, add the remaining 2 tablespoons butter to the skillet. Use a wooden spoon to scrape any bits from the bottom of the skillet. Stir in lemon juice, capers, and parsley; simmer 1 minute. Pour sauce over chicken.

PLAN AHEAD: Pound the chicken breast halves when you bring them home from the grocery store. Place in a freezer bag and freeze up to 2 months. Defrost completely in refrigerator.

Santa Fe Chicken

RED AND YELLOW BELL PEPPERS AND ORANGE
CHEDDAR CHEESE MAKE A COLORFUL ENTRÉE.
IT'S PERFECT WHEN COOKING FOR CROWDS—
YOU CAN LOAD A LOT OF CHICKEN BREASTS
ONTO ONE BAKING SHEET.

SIDES: Fresh Chunky Tomato Salsa
(page 210) and tortilla chips.

DESSERT: Chocolate ice cream
sundaes.

MAKES: 6 servings

Nonstick cooking spray

6   medium boneless, skinless
    chicken breast halves
    (2¼ pounds total)

¼   cup olive oil

2   teaspoons chili powder

1   teaspoon salt

½   teaspoon black pepper

1   red bell pepper, thinly sliced

1   yellow bell pepper, thinly sliced

1   medium red onion, cut into
    ¼-inch slices

2   tablespoons freshly squeezed
    lemon juice

1   7-ounce can whole green
    chile peppers, drained and
    cut into strips

1½ cups shredded cheddar cheese

ONE Preheat oven to 375°F. Coat a large baking sheet
with cooking spray.

TWO Lightly brush each chicken breast half with
some of the oil; sprinkle with chili powder, salt,
and black pepper. Arrange chicken breasts on the
prepared baking sheet. Bake, uncovered, about
20 minutes or until chicken is no longer pink.

THREE Meanwhile, preheat the remaining oil in a
large skillet. Saute the bell peppers and onion in
hot oil about 3 minutes or until vegetables are just
tender. Remove skillet from heat. Pour lemon juice
over vegetables; toss to coat.

FOUR Top each chicken breast half with chile pepper
strips, vegetable mixture, and cheese.

FIVE Bake, uncovered, about 5 minutes or until
cheese melts.

PLAN AHEAD: Prepare through Step Two up to 1 day
ahead. Cover and refrigerate. Preheat oven. Continue
according to Step Three.

FREEZE AHEAD: Prepare through Step Four. Cover
with plastic wrap and foil. Freeze up to 2 months.
Defrost completely in refrigerator. Preheat oven.
Remove plastic wrap and foil and continue according
to Step Five.

Curried Chicken and Rice Salad

THIS HEARTY SALAD CAN BE SERVED FOR LUNCH OR SUPPER. THIS WAS ONE OF MY SON'S FAVORITE DISHES WHEN HE WAS GROWING UP. THE RAISINS WORK WITH THE ONIONS AND OTHER SAVORY FLAVORS TO CREATE A SWEET-AND-SOUR EDGE.

SIDE: Parmesan Toast (page 163).

DESSERT: Cream Cheese Cupcakes (page 244).

MAKES: 6 servings

- 3 cups cooked rice
- 2 medium boneless, skinless chicken breast halves (12 ounces total), poached (see pages 7-8) and chopped (2 cups)
- 1 green bell pepper, thinly sliced
- 1 roasted red bell pepper, chopped
- ¼ cup finely chopped fresh parsley
- 3 green onions, thinly sliced
- 2 tablespoons raisins
- 1 recipe Curried Salad Dressing

ONE In a large bowl combine rice, chopped chicken, green bell pepper, roasted red pepper, parsley, green onions, and raisins. Pour Curried Salad Dressing over chicken mixture; toss to coat.

PLAN AHEAD: Prepare salad up to 2 days ahead. Cover and refrigerate.

CURRIED SALAD DRESSING: In a bowl whisk together ½ cup cider vinegar, 3 tablespoons freshly squeezed lemon juice, 1 tablespoon sugar, 1 teaspoon minced fresh garlic, ½ teaspoon curry powder, ½ teaspoon salt, and ¼ teaspoon black pepper. Drizzle in ½ cup vegetable oil, whisking constantly.

Orange-Tarragon-Glazed Baked Chicken

ORANGE JUICE CONCENTRATE ADDS AN INTENSE ORANGE FLAVOR BALANCED PERFECTLY BY ONIONS AND TARRAGON.

SIDE: Fruit and Nut Couscous (page 175).

DESSERT: New York-style cheesecake.

MAKES: 6 servings

- 6 medium boneless, skinless chicken breast halves (2¼ pounds total)
- 1 cup orange juice concentrate, thawed
- ½ cup finely chopped onion
- 2 tablespoons vegetable oil
- 1 tablespoon dried tarragon, crushed
- 1 teaspoon salt

ONE Place chicken in a resealable plastic bag. For marinade, combine orange juice concentrate, onion, oil, tarragon, and salt; pour over chicken in bag. Seal bag; turn to coat chicken. Refrigerate for 2 hours.

TWO Preheat oven to 350°F. Drain chicken, discarding marinade. Arrange chicken in a 13×9×2-inch baking dish. Bake, uncovered, about 20 minutes or until no longer pink.

FREEZE AHEAD: Prepare through Step One. Freeze up to 2 months. Defrost completely in refrigerator. Continue according to Step Two.

ORANGE-TARRAGON–GLAZED GRILLED CHICKEN: Prepare according to Step One. Preheat grill to medium heat. Grill chicken about 20 minutes or until no longer pink, turning once halfway through grilling.

Asian Chicken en Papillote

THE PACKETS ARE LIKE LITTLE PRESENTS FOR EVERYONE.

SIDE: Pecan Wild Rice Pilaf (page 154).

DESSERT: Neopolitan ice cream served with chocolate-filled sugar wafer cookies.

MAKES: 6 servings

¼ cup hoisin sauce

1 teaspoon grated fresh ginger

1 teaspoon minced fresh garlic

2 cups fresh broccoli florets

2 cups fresh snow peas, trimmed

2 cups sliced celery

2 cups packaged peeled fresh baby carrots

1 cup sliced fresh mushrooms

1 cup sliced water chestnuts

¼ cup sliced green onion

6 12-inch squares of foil

6 boneless, skinless chicken breast halves (2¼ pounds total)

ONE Preheat oven to 375°F.

TWO In a large bowl combine hoisin sauce, ginger, and garlic. Add broccoli, snow peas, celery, carrots, mushrooms, water chestnuts, and green onion; toss to coat.

THREE Place one square of foil on the counter; place one chicken breast half in the center. Top chicken with 1½ cups of the vegetable mixture. Bring up two opposite sides of foil; seal with a double fold. Double-fold the remaining ends to seal packet. Repeat with remaining squares of foil, chicken, and vegetable mixture.

FOUR Place packets on a large baking sheet. Bake about 30 minutes or until chicken is no longer pink. Let packets rest a few minutes before opening to avoid hot steam.

Chinese Chicken Jade Salad

I CONCOCTED THIS RECIPE AFTER ENJOYING A SIMILAR SALAD WHILE IN NASHVILLE ON A GIRLFRIEND TRIP. I CRAVED THE COMBINATION OF VINEGAR, SUGAR, AND GINGER AND THE CRUNCH OF PEANUTS AND CABBAGE. NOW WE CAN ALL MAKE IT ANYTIME.

SIDE: Pita chips.

DESSERT: Caramel Pound Cake: Drizzle slices of purchased pound cake with caramel topping. Dollop with whipped dessert topping.

MAKES: 6 servings

3 medium boneless, skinless chicken breast halves (18 ounces total), poached (see pages 7-8) and chopped (3 cups)

1 medium head napa cabbage, shredded

2 cups honey-roasted peanuts or cashews

5 green onions, thinly sliced

Red bell peppers (optional)

¼ cup vegetable oil

3 tablespoons rice vinegar

2 tablespoons sugar

1 tablespoon toasted sesame oil

1½ teaspoons dry mustard

1 teaspoon soy sauce

1 teaspoon grated fresh ginger

1 cup crispy Chinese noodles

ONE In a large bowl combine chopped chicken, cabbage, peanuts, green onion, and, if desired, red bell peppers. For dressing, in a jar with a tight-fitting lid combine vegetable oil, vinegar, sugar, sesame oil, mustard, soy sauce, and ginger. Cover and shake well.

TWO Pour dressing over chicken mixture; toss to coat. Sprinkle with noodles; toss to combine.

Turkey Tenderloins with Fresh Cranberry-Orange Compote

TENDERLOIN IS THE PERFECT CUT OF TURKEY. YOU DON'T HAVE TO COOK THE WHOLE BIRD, AND WITH NO BONES THERE IS NO WASTE.

SIDE: Corn Bread Dressing (page 167).

DESSERT: Pumpkin pie.

MAKES: 6 servings

Nonstick cooking spray

3   turkey breast tenderloins (about 1½ pounds total)

3   teaspoons dried thyme, crushed

1½ teaspoons seasoned salt

3   slices bacon

1   recipe Fresh Cranberry-Orange Compote (page 221)

ONE Preheat oven to 350°F. Coat a 9×9-inch baking dish with cooking spray.

TWO Place tenderloins in prepared baking dish; sprinkle each with 1 teaspoon of the thyme and ½ teaspoon of the seasoned salt. Cover each tenderloin with 1 slice of bacon. Bake, uncovered, about 40 minutes or until internal temperature reads 165°F.

THREE To serve, cut each turkey tenderloin into ½-inch slices. Serve with warm Fresh Cranberry-Orange Compote.

PLAN AHEAD: Prepare Fresh Cranberry-Orange Compote up to 3 days ahead. Cover and refrigerate. Reheat over low heat.

seafood

Crab Dip Divine

I FIRST TASTED THIS DIP AT A FANCY AFFAIR IN DALLAS. I WANTED TO JUMP INTO THE CHAFING DISH AND SWIM AROUND IN IT. ALAS, THE CATERERS WOULDN'T GIVE ME THE RECIPE. AFTER MANY TRIALS, THIS IS WHAT DEVELOPED.

SEAFOOD

SIDE: Endive and Apple Salad (page 194).

DESSERT: Shortbread dipped in chocolate.

MAKES: 12 to 15 servings

- 4 cups mayonnaise
- 2 cups shredded cheddar cheese
- 1 cup chopped green onion
- ½ cup salsa
- ½ cup sliced pitted black olives
- 1 tablespoon chili powder
- ½ teaspoon ground cumin
- 1 6-ounce can crabmeat, drained and flaked

  Tortilla chips and/or assorted crackers

ONE Preheat oven to 350°F. Stir together mayonnaise, cheese, green onion, salsa, olives, chili powder, and cumin. Stir in crabmeat. Transfer to a 2-quart baking dish.

TWO Bake, uncovered, for 15 to 20 minutes or just until warm. (Don't overheat or mixture will separate.) Serve with chips or crackers.

PLAN AHEAD: Prepare through Step One 1 day ahead. Cover and refrigerate. Preheat oven. Uncover and continue according to Step Two.

SEAFOOD DIP DIVINE: Prepare as directed, except substitute lobster, whitefish, or salmon for the crabmeat.

Crab and Artichoke Pasta

CRABMEAT AND ARTICHOKE HEARTS MAKE THIS DISH SEEM EXTRAVAGANT, BUT IT IS REALLY EASY TO MAKE.

SIDES: Green peas and Spinach Salad (page 196).

DESSERT: Chocolate Sheet Cake with Chocolate Icing (page 246).

MAKES: 4 to 6 servings

Nonstick cooking spray

- 1 cup dried shell macaroni
- 2 tablespoons butter
- 2 tablespoons all-purpose flour
- ½ teaspoon salt
- ¼ teaspoon white pepper
- 2 cups milk
- 1 pound fresh lump crabmeat or two 6-ounce cans crabmeat, drained and flaked
- 1 15-ounce can artichoke hearts, drained and chopped
- 1 tablespoon grated onion
- ½ cup shredded cheddar cheese

ONE Preheat oven to 350°F. Coat a 13×9×2-inch baking dish with cooking spray.

TWO Cook the pasta according to package directions; drain.

THREE Melt butter in a large skillet over medium-high heat; whisk in flour, salt, and pepper. Cook and whisk for 1 minute. Remove skillet from heat; whisk in milk until smooth. Return skillet to heat; simmer 1 minute, whisking constantly.

FOUR Stir in crabmeat, cooked macaroni, artichoke hearts, and onion. Transfer to prepared baking dish. Sprinkle with cheese.

FIVE Bake, uncovered, about 30 minutes or until hot and bubbly.

PLAN AHEAD: Prepare through Step Four up to 2 days ahead. Cover and refrigerate. Preheat oven. Uncover and continue according to Step Five.

FREEZE AHEAD: Prepare through Step Four. Cover with plastic wrap and foil. Freeze up to 1 month. Defrost completely in refrigerator. Preheat oven. Remove plastic wrap and foil and continue according to Step Five.

Chef Jon Bonnell's Lump Crab Cakes

CHEF JON BONNELL IS AN INSTRUCTOR AT OUR COOKING SCHOOL, THE CULINARY SCHOOL OF FORT WORTH. HE WAS NAMED A RISING STAR OF AMERICAN CUISINE BY THE JAMES BEARD FOUNDATION AND HAS BEEN INVITED TO COOK AT THE FAMED JAMES BEARD HOUSE TWICE. JON SERVES THESE CRAB CAKES AT HIS RESTAURANT, BONNELL'S RESTAURANT.

SIDES: Steamed asparagus and Parmesan Toast (page 163).

DESSERT: Baked Fruit (page 237).

MAKES: 6 to 8 servings

- 2 eggs, beaten
- 1 cup chopped green onion (green parts only)
- ½ cup diced red bell pepper
- ½ cup mayonnaise
- 1 tablespoon Dijon mustard
- 1 tablespoon Worcestershire sauce
- 1 tablespoon bottled hot sauce (optional)
- 1 teaspoon Creole seasoning (or to taste)
- 2 pounds fresh lump crabmeat
- 1½ cups panko bread crumbs
- 2 tablespoons olive oil
- 2 tablespoons butter
- 1 recipe Green Onion and Lime Aioli

ONE In a large bowl combine eggs, green onion, bell pepper, mayonnaise, mustard, Worcestershire sauce, hot pepper sauce (if desired), and Creole seasoning. Add crabmeat; mix well. Shape crab mixture into 12 patties. Press bread crumbs into both sides of each crab cake.

TWO Preheat oil and butter in a large skillet over medium-low heat. Cook crab cakes in hot oil and butter until golden brown, turning once. Serve with Green Onion and Lime Aioli.

FREEZE AHEAD: Prepare through Step One. Place in a freezer container and freeze up to 1 month. Defrost completely in refrigerator. Continue according to Step Two.

GREEN ONION AND LIME AIOLI: In a food processor combine 1 cup chopped green onion, ½ cup freshly squeezed lime juice, 2 tablespoons Dijon mustard, 2 egg yolks, 1 teaspoon salt, and ½ teaspoon black pepper. Cover and process until combined. With machine running, slowly pour in 2 cups vegetable oil. Process until thick and creamy. Makes about 2½ cups.

Pecan-Crusted Salmon Cakes

THIS IS ONE OF SUPER SUPPERS' MOST REQUESTED DISHES. WE LOVE THE NEW FOIL PACKETS OF SALMON, BUT YOU CAN USE CANNED AS WELL.

SIDE: Caesar Salad (page 193).

DESSERT: Strawberry sorbet.

MAKES: 6 servings

- 1 cup cracker crumbs
- ½ cup finely chopped pecans
- 1 teaspoon salt
- 1 teaspoon minced fresh garlic
- ½ teaspoon black pepper
- 2 eggs
- ¼ cup diced onion
- 2 tablespoons freshly squeezed lemon juice
- 2 tablespoons dried parsley flakes
- 1½ pounds canned salmon, drained
- 2 tablespoons buttermilk
- 1 tablespoon vegetable oil
- 1 recipe Quick-and-Easy Dill Sauce
- 1 recipe Tartar Sauce

ONE For crust, in a shallow dish combine ½ cup of the cracker crumbs, pecans, salt, garlic, and pepper. Set aside.

TWO In a large bowl combine the remaining ½ cup cracker crumbs, 1 of the eggs, onion, lemon juice, and parsley. Add salmon; mix well. Shape salmon mixture into 6 patties.

THREE In a small bowl beat together the remaining egg and buttermilk; brush each salmon cake with some of the egg mixture. Press crust mixture into both sides of each salmon cake.

FOUR Preheat oil in a large skillet over medium-low heat. Cook salmon cakes in hot oil until golden brown, turning once. Serve with Quick-and-Easy Dill Sauce or Tartar Sauce.

FREEZE AHEAD: Prepare through Step Three. Place in a flat freezer container and freeze up to 1 month. Defrost completely in refrigerator. Continue according to Step Four.

QUICK-AND-EASY DILL SAUCE: In a bowl combine 2 cups sour cream, ¼ cup freshly squeezed lemon juice, and 1 tablespoon chopped fresh dill or 2 teaspoons dried dill. Season to taste with salt and black pepper. Cover and refrigerate until serving time. Makes about 2 cups.

TARTAR SAUCE: In a bowl combine 1 cup mayonnaise, 2 tablespoons sweet pickle relish, 2 tablespoons grated onion, 1 tablespoon freshly squeezed lemon juice, ½ teaspoon salt, and a dash of cayenne pepper or bottled hot pepper sauce. Cover and refrigerate until serving time. Makes about 1 cup.

Crunchy Baked Asian Tilapia

WE HAVE NUMEROUS REQUESTS FOR THIS DISH AT SUPER SUPPERS. YOU CAN SUBSTITUTE OTHER WHITEFISH.

SIDE: Stir-Fried Bok Choy (page 205).

DESSERT: Paradise Sundaes: Top ice cream with drained pineapple chunks, shredded coconut, and chopped nuts.

MAKES: 6 servings

Nonstick cooking spray

¼ cup Dijon mustard

2 tablespoons hoisin sauce

1½ cups panko bread crumbs

6 4-ounce tilapia fillets

ONE Preheat oven to 375°F. Coat a baking sheet with cooking spray.

TWO Stir together mustard and hoisin sauce. Place panko bread crumbs in a shallow dish. Brush both sides of fish fillets with mustard mixture. Coat both sides of fish fillets with bread crumbs.

THREE Place fillets on prepared baking sheet. Bake, uncovered, about 30 minutes or until fish is flaky.

FREEZE AHEAD: Prepare through Step Two. Place in a freezer container and freeze up to 1 month. Defrost completely in refrigerator. Preheat oven. Continue according to Step Three.

Fish Tacos with Chili Aioli

CHILI AIOLI IS THE KILLER INGREDIENT IN THESE TACOS. AIOLI IS TRADITIONALLY A GARLICKY MAYONNAISE, BUT IN THIS RECIPE IT IS CHANGED A BIT.

SIDES: Fresh Chunky Tomato Salsa (page 210) and Chef Duane's Spanish Rice (page 158).

DESSERT: Vanilla bean ice cream.

MAKES: 6 servings

- 1 tablespoon chili powder
- 2 teaspoons seasoned salt
- 1 pound fish fillets (such as tilapia, cod, rockfish, or catfish)
- 2 tablespoons olive oil
- 1 tablespoon butter
- 6 7-inch flour tortillas
- 2 cups shredded lettuce
- Salsa
- Fresh cilantro
- 1 cup shredded cheddar cheese (optional)
- 1 recipe Chili Aioli
- Lime wedges (optional)

ONE Stir together chili powder and salt; sprinkle evenly over both sides of each fish fillet.

TWO Preheat oil and butter in a large skillet over medium heat. Add fish in a single layer; fry fish for 1 minute. Turn carefully; fry 2 to 3 minutes more or until fish is flaky.

THREE Coarsely cut up the fried fish. Fill each tortilla with fish, lettuce, salsa, cilantro, and, if desired, cheddar cheese. Top with Chili Aioli. If desired, squeeze limes over filling.

PLAN AHEAD: Prepare fish through Step Two and prepare Chili Aioli up to 2 days ahead. Cover and refrigerate. Reheat fish in skillet. Continue according to Step Three.

FREEZE AHEAD: Prepare through Step One. Place in a freezer container and freeze up to 1 month. Defrost completely in refrigerator. Continue according to Step Two.

CHILI AIOLI: Stir together 1 cup mayonnaise, 1 tablespoon chili powder, 1 tablespoon freshly squeezed lemon juice, and 1 teaspoon ground cumin. Cover and refrigerate up to 2 days. Makes about 1 cup.

113

Seared Tilapia with Lemon-Tarragon-Mustard Sauce

WE LOVE THE MILD FLAVOR OF TILAPIA. IT PROVIDES A PERFECT BASE FOR TANGY SAUCES LIKE THIS ONE WITH LEMON AND MUSTARD.

SIDE: Steamed Broccoli Salad with Pine Nuts and Raisins (page 180).

DESSERT: Strawberry Cream Cheese Angel Food Cake (page 245).

MAKES: 4 servings

1½	**pounds tilapia fillets**
1	**teaspoon seasoned salt**
2	**tablespoons olive oil**
1	**tablespoon butter**
½	**cup freshly squeezed lemon juice**
¼	**cup dry white wine or chicken broth**
1	**tablespoon Dijon mustard**
1	**tablespoon chopped fresh tarragon**

ONE Sprinkle both sides of fish with seasoned salt. Preheat oil and butter in a large skillet over medium heat. Add fish in a single layer; fry fish for 1 minute. Turn carefully; fry for 2 to 3 minutes more or until fish is flaky. Transfer fish to a serving platter; keep warm.

TWO For sauce, add lemon juice and wine to skillet. Use a wooden spoon to scrape up any bits in the skillet. Whisk in mustard; simmer for 2 minutes. Stir in tarragon. Pour sauce over fish.

FREEZE AHEAD: Freeze fresh tilapia fillets up to 1 month. Defrost completely in refrigerator.

Tex-Mex Catfish

TOMATILLOS LOOK LIKE GREEN TOMATOES AND ARE MILDLY TART WITH A HINT OF LIME FLAVOR. THEY ARE OFTEN USED IN MEXICAN COOKING TO MAKE GREEN SAUCES.

SIDES: Refried beans, salsa and chips, and a salad of shredded lettuce and chopped tomatoes.

DESSERT: Instant Sopaipillas (page 231).

MAKES: 4 to 6 servings

Nonstick cooking spray

6 4-ounce catfish fillets

¾ cup chunky salsa

¾ cup canned tomatillos, drained and chopped

1 tablespoon chopped fresh cilantro

1 tablespoon freshly squeezed lime juice

1 teaspoon salt

½ teaspoon ground cumin

½ teaspoon black pepper

ONE Preheat oven to 350°F. Coat a 13×9×2-inch baking dish with cooking spray.

TWO Place catfish fillets in prepared baking dish. In a bowl stir together salsa, tomatillos, cilantro, lime juice, salt, cumin, and pepper; pour over fillets.

THREE Bake, uncovered, about 35 minutes or until fish is flaky.

PLAN AHEAD: Prepare through Step Two up to 2 days ahead. Cover and refrigerate. Preheat oven. Uncover and continue according to Step Three.

FREEZE AHEAD: Prepare through Step Two. Cover with plastic wrap and foil. Freeze up to 1 month. Defrost completely in refrigerator. Preheat oven. Remove plastic wrap and foil and continue according to Step Three.

Fish in a Flash

THE DRIED HERB MIXTURE CONTAINS A GREAT BLEND OF FLAVORS.

SIDES: Parsley couscous, asparagus, and sliced tomatoes.

DESSERT: Lemon Blueberry Pudding: Top instant lemon pudding with fresh blueberries or blueberry pie filling.

MAKES: 6 servings

- ½ cup panko bread crumbs
- 2 teaspoons dried parsley flakes
- 1 teaspoon dried minced onion
- 1 teaspoon garlic powder
- 1 teaspoon dried basil, crushed
- ½ teaspoon salt
- ½ teaspoon lemon-pepper seasoning
- ¼ teaspoon cayenne pepper
- 6 4-ounce whitefish fillets (such as tilapia, cod, or sole)
- ¼ cup vegetable oil

ONE In a shallow dish stir together bread crumbs, parsley flakes, onion, garlic powder, basil, salt, lemon-pepper seasoning, and cayenne pepper. Brush both sides of fish fillets with 2 tablespoons of the oil. Coat both sides of fish fillets with bread crumb mixture.

TWO Preheat the remaining 2 tablespoons oil in a large skillet over medium heat. Add fish in a single layer; fry fish for 1 minute. Turn carefully; fry 2 to 3 minutes more or until fish is flaky.

FREEZE AHEAD: Prepare through Step One. Place in a freezer container and freeze up to 1 month. Defrost completely in refrigerator. Continue according to Step Two.

Seafood Divan

USE YOUR FAVORITE SEAFOOD. YOU COULD EVEN USE CANNED TUNA OR SALMON.

SIDES: Tossed green salad and Bruschetta (page 168).

DESSERT: Frozen Adobe Pie (page 239).

MAKES: 6 servings

- 3 cups fresh broccoli florets
- 2 tablespoons water
  Nonstick cooking spray
- ¼ cup butter
- ½ cup chopped onion
- ¼ cup chopped red bell pepper
- ¼ cup all-purpose flour
- 1 cup chicken broth
- 1 cup milk
- ¼ cup dry white wine
- 2½ cups shredded cheddar cheese
- 1 teaspoon salt
- ½ teaspoon black pepper
- 1 pound whitefish fillets
- ¼ pound peeled and deveined small uncooked shrimp
- ¼ pound small uncooked scallops

ONE To steam broccoli, place in a microwave-safe bowl; sprinkle with water. Cover and microwave on 100% power (high) for 2 minutes. Stir; microwave about 2 minutes more or until just tender. Set aside.

TWO Preheat oven to 350°F. Coat a 13×9×2-inch baking dish with cooking spray.

THREE For sauce, in a large skillet melt butter over medium heat. Saute onion and bell pepper until tender. Add flour; cook and stir 1 minute. Slowly whisk in chicken broth, milk, and wine. Cook and whisk until thickened. Stir in ½ cup of the cheese, salt, and black pepper. Remove skillet from heat.

FOUR Spread steamed broccoli in prepared baking dish. Top with fillets, shrimp, and scallops. Pour sauce evenly over the top.

FIVE Bake, covered, 45 minutes. Uncover; sprinkle with the remaining 2 cups cheese. Bake about 10 minutes more or until fish is flaky, seafood is cooked through, and cheese is melted.

PLAN AHEAD: Prepare through Step Four up to 2 days ahead. Cover and refrigerate. Preheat oven. Continue according to Step Five.

Poached Salmon

POACHED SALMON MAKES A GREAT DINNER, AND ANY LEFTOVERS CAN BE CHILLED AND SERVED OVER SALAD THE NEXT DAY. FOR A FANCY HORS D'OEUVRE, SERVE CRACKERS WITH A POACHED SALMON HALF ON A LARGE PLATTER. COVER SALMON WITH PAPER-THIN CUCUMBER SLICES TO REPRESENT SCALES.

SIDES: Steamed asparagus drizzled with olive oil and lemon and Pastina Risotto (page 176).

DESSERT: Easy Apple Crisp (page 233).

MAKES: 6 servings

1½	cups dry white wine
1½	cups water
1	lemon, sliced
1	small onion, sliced
1	bay leaf
6	whole peppercorns
1	teaspoon salt
½	teaspoon black pepper
1	3-pound salmon fillet
1	recipe Cucumber Raita

ONE In a fish poacher or large skillet combine wine, water, lemon, onion, bay leaf, peppercorns, salt, and pepper. Bring to boiling.

TWO Add salmon to poacher or skillet (if using a skillet, you may need to cut salmon into smaller pieces). Turn heat to low. Cover and simmer gently about 8 minutes or until fish is flaky. Carefully remove salmon; place on a serving platter. Serve with Cucumber Raita.

FREEZE AHEAD: Place wine mixture and salmon in a freezer bag and freeze up to 1 month. Defrost completely in refrigerator. Continue according to Step Two.

CUCUMBER RAITA: Peel, seed, and coarsely grate 3 cucumbers. Place grated cucumbers in a colander; sprinkle with 1 teaspoon salt. Let stand 30 minutes to release juices; drain well. Transfer cucumbers to a large bowl. Stir in 1 cup nonfat plain yogurt, 2 tablespoons finely chopped fresh herbs (such as dill, cilantro, and/or mint), 2 teaspoons freshly squeezed lemon juice, ½ teaspoon black pepper, and 1 clove garlic, minced. Cover and refrigerate until serving time. Makes about 4 cups.

Pesto Salmon and Vegetables en Papillote

PESTO AND VEGETABLES STEAM WITH SALMON INSIDE PARCHMENT PAPER PACKETS, SEASONING THE FISH PERFECTLY AND CREATING A BEAUTIFUL PRESENTATION.

SIDE: Pecan Wild Rice Pilaf (page 154).

DESSERT: My Mom's Strawberry Cake (page 242).

MAKES: 6 servings

6	small new potatoes, sliced
1	pound fresh green beans
6	12-inch squares of parchment paper
6	6-ounce salmon fillets
6	thin slices lemon
6	tablespoons prepared pesto
6	tablespoons shredded carrot
6	tablespoons sliced green onion
6	tablespoons sliced, pitted black olives
1½	teaspoons dried thyme, crushed

ONE Fill a medium saucepan ⅔ full with cold water; bring to boiling. Cook potatoes and beans 5 to 7 minutes until almost tender, remove and cool.

TWO Preheat oven to 350°F. Place one square of paper on the counter; divide potatoes and beans evenly among papers; place one salmon fillet in the center. Top each with one lemon slice and 1 tablespoon each of pesto, carrot, green onion, and olives. Sprinkle each with ¾ teaspoon thyme.

THREE Bring up two opposite sides of paper; seal with a double fold. Double-fold the remaining ends to seal packets.

FOUR Place packets on a large baking sheet. Bake for 25 minutes or until fish is flak.y. Let packets rest a few minutes before opening to avoid hot steam.

PLAN AHEAD: Prepare through Step Two up to 6 hours ahead; refrigerate. Continue according to Step Three.

FREEZE AHEAD: Prepare through Step Two. Place packets on a baking sheet. Cover with foil and freeze up to 1 month. Defrost completely in refrigerator. Preheat oven. Remove foil and continue according to Step Three.

Fish Fillets with Lemon and Capers

THIS DISH IS ELEGANT AND DRESSY, YET SO EASY YOU CAN SERVE IT AS OFTEN AS YOU LIKE.

SEAFOOD

SIDES: Steamed Broccoli Salad with Pine Nuts and Raisins (page 180) and Apricot-Glazed Carrots (page 212).

DESSERT: Butterscotch Sundaes: Top vanilla or chocolate ice cream with butterscotch sauce.

MAKES: 4 servings

1¾	to 2 pounds fish fillets (such as halibut, cod, salmon, sole, or flounder)
1	teaspoon salt
1	teaspoon black pepper
⅓	cup all-purpose flour
1	tablespoon olive oil
¼	cup freshly squeezed lemon juice
2	tablespoons lemon zest
3	tablespoons butter, cut up
¼	cup finely chopped fresh parsley
1	tablespoon capers

ONE Season both sides of fish fillets with salt and pepper. Place flour in a shallow dish. Coat both sides of fish fillets with flour.

TWO Preheat oil in a large skillet over medium heat. Add fish in a single layer; fry for 1 minute. Turn carefully; fry 2 to 3 minutes more or until fish is flaky. Remove fish from skillet; keep warm.

THREE Add lemon juice and lemon zest to skillet. Stir in butter, a little at a time. Add parsley and capers. Return fillets to skillet; heat through.

FREEZE AHEAD: Keep fish fillets in the freezer up to 3 months. Defrost completely in refrigerator and prepare according to Step One.

Shrimp Scampi

THE FIRST TIME I TASTED SHRIMP SCAMPI WAS IN A RESTAURANT IN CALIFORNIA IN 1965. I WENT HOME AND MADE UP THIS VERSION.

SIDES: Spinach Salad (page 196) and Lemon Parmesan Risotto (page 155).

DESSERT: Fishbowl Trifle (page 248).

MAKES: 4 to 6 servings

- 2 pounds peeled and deveined uncooked large shrimp
- 1 cup butter, melted
- ¼ cup olive oil
- 3 tablespoons freshly squeezed lemon juice
- 2 tablespoons chopped fresh basil
- 1 teaspoon minced fresh garlic
- 1 teaspoon dried oregano, crushed
- ¾ teaspoon salt
- ¼ teaspoon white pepper

ONE Preheat oven to 450°F.

TWO Cut each shrimp lengthwise along the underside, being careful not to cut all the way through. Spread shrimp open, butterfly fashion, in a broiler-proof 13×9×2-inch baking dish.

THREE Combine melted butter and olive oil; stir in lemon juice, basil, garlic, oregano, salt, and pepper. Pour over shrimp.

FOUR Bake, uncovered, 8 minutes. Turn oven to broil. Broil shrimp about 3 minutes or until shrimp are opaque and mixture is sizzling.

FREEZE AHEAD: Prepare through Step Three. Cover with plastic wrap and foil. Freeze up to 2 weeks. Defrost completely in refrigerator. Preheat oven. Remove plastic wrap and foil and continue according to Step Four.

Shrimp in Cheese Sauce

WHAT COULD BE MORE DECADENT THAN SHRIMP IN A CREAMY CHEESE SAUCE?

SIDE: Italian Green Beans and Potatoes (page 214).

DESSERT: Baked Fruit (page 237).

MAKES: 4 to 6 servings

- 1 15-ounce can diced tomatoes
- 2 tablespoons butter
- 1½ cups thinly sliced green onion
- 1½ cups chopped celery
- 1½ cups chopped bell pepper
- 1 2-pound package process cheese product, cut up
- 2 pounds peeled and deveined cooked shrimp

  Toast, rice, or noodles

ONE Drain tomatoes, reserving juice; set aside.

TWO For sauce, melt butter in a large skillet. Saute green onion, celery, and bell pepper in hot butter until tender. Stir in drained tomatoes and cheese, stirring until cheese melts and sauce is smooth. (Add reserved tomato juice to make a smooth sauce, if needed.)

THREE Add shrimp; heat through. Serve over toast, rice, or noodles.

PLAN AHEAD: Prepare through Step Two 1 day ahead. Cover and refrigerate. Reheat over very low heat. Continue according to Step Three.

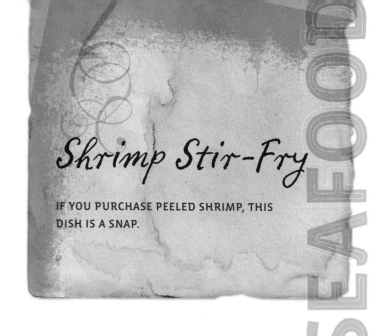

Shrimp Stir-Fry

IF YOU PURCHASE PEELED SHRIMP, THIS DISH IS A SNAP.

SIDES: Steamed rice or crispy Chinese noodles and sliced fresh pineapple.

DESSERT: Apricot Carrot Cake: Drizzle sliced carrot cake with warm apricot preserves.

MAKES: 6 servings

- 2 tablespoons seasoned stir-fry oil or vegetable oil
- 1 cup packaged peeled fresh baby carrots
- 1 cup small fresh broccoli florets
- 1 pound peeled and deveined uncooked shrimp
- ½ cup hoisin sauce
- ¼ cup soy sauce
- 2 tablespoons toasted sesame oil
- 2 tablespoons rice vinegar
- 1 tablespoon minced fresh garlic
- 1 tablespoon grated fresh ginger
- ½ teaspoon red pepper flakes (optional)

ONE In a wok or large skillet preheat stir-fry oil over high heat. Add carrots and broccoli; stir-fry for 3 minutes. Add shrimp; stir-fry for 1 minute more.

TWO Meanwhile, for sauce, stir together hoisin sauce, soy sauce, sesame oil, rice vinegar, garlic, ginger, and, if desired, red pepper flakes. Add sauce to wok; stir-fry about 2 minutes more or until shrimp are opaque and sauce is simmering.

Mediterranean Shrimp and 5-Bean Salad

THIS ATTRACTIVE SALAD USES CANNED BEANS AND VEGETABLES, WHICH MEANS YOU CAN KEEP THE INGREDIENTS ON HAND AND WHIP IT UP ON SHORT NOTICE.

SIDE: Rosemary focaccia.

DESSERT: Hello Dolly Bars (page 229).

MAKES: 6 to 8 servings

- 1 pound peeled and deveined cooked shrimp
- 1 cup whole pitted black olives
- ½ cup canned red kidney beans
- ⅓ cup canned green beans
- ½ cup canned garbanzo beans
- ½ cup canned wax beans
- ½ cup canned white navy beans
- ½ cup chopped tomato
- ½ cup quartered artichoke hearts
- 3 tablespoons olive oil
- 2 tablespoons freshly squeezed lemon juice
- 1 teaspoon dried oregano, crushed
- 1 teaspoon salt
- 1 teaspoon minced fresh garlic
- ½ teaspoon black pepper
- ½ cup crumbled feta cheese

ONE In a large bowl stir together shrimp, olives, kidney beans, green beans, garbanzo beans, wax beans, navy beans, tomato, artichoke hearts, oil, lemon juice, oregano, salt, garlic, and pepper. Cover and refrigerate until serving time.

TWO Just before serving, add feta cheese; toss to combine.

FREEZE AHEAD: Place all ingredients except feta cheese in a freezer bag and freeze up to 2 months. Defrost completely in refrigerator. Continue according to Step Two.

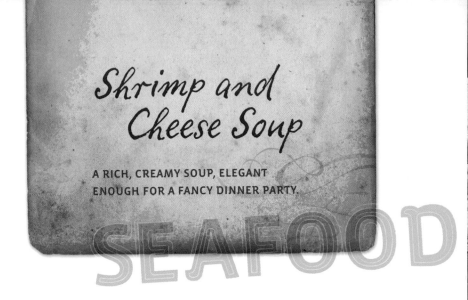

Shrimp and Cheese Soup

A RICH, CREAMY SOUP, ELEGANT ENOUGH FOR A FANCY DINNER PARTY.

SEAFOOD

SIDES: Bruschetta (page 168).

DESSERT: Chocolate-Drizzled Cream Puffs: Drizzle chocolate syrup over purchased cream puffs.

MAKES: 6 to 8 servings

- 2 cups chicken broth
- 2 cups chopped onion
- 2 cups chopped carrot
- 2 cups chopped celery
- 2 cups diced potato
- 8 cups milk
- ½ cup butter, melted
- ½ cup cornstarch
- 1 2-pound package process cheese product, cut up
- 1 pound peeled and deveined cooked shrimp
- 1 teaspoon salt (or to taste)
- ½ teaspoon black pepper

ONE Place chicken broth in a large soup pot. Add onion, carrot, celery, and potato. Simmer until vegetables are tender. Stir in milk; return to simmering.

TWO Meanwhile, in a large bowl stir together melted butter and cornstarch to make a paste. Slowly whisk in 3 cups of the hot milk mixture. Add cornstarch mixture to soup pot, whisking to combine. Simmer soup for 1 minute, whisking constantly.

THREE Add cheese to soup pot, stirring until cheese melts and soup is smooth. Stir in shrimp, salt, and pepper; heat through.

PLAN AHEAD: Prepare through Step Two up to 2 days ahead. Cover and refrigerate. Reheat over very low heat. Continue according to Step Three.

vegetarian

Chinese Noodles

EIGHT SERVINGS MIGHT BE ONLY ENOUGH FOR TWO PEOPLE IF YOU LOVE THIS DISH AS MUCH AS I DO. ANY LEFTOVERS ARE GREAT COLD, RIGHT OUT OF THE REFRIGERATOR. EATING NOODLES IS JUST PLAIN FUN.

VEGETARIAN

SIDE: Vegetable spring rolls.

DESSERT: Fortune cookies dipped halfway in melted chocolate.

MAKES: 8 servings

- 8 cups water
- 1 tablespoon salt
- 1 pound dried Chinese egg noodles or angel hair pasta
- 2 tablespoons sesame seeds
- ¼ cup vegetable oil
- 2 tablespoons toasted sesame oil
- ¾ cup soy sauce
- 3 tablespoons ground coriander
- 1 teaspoon salt
- ¼ teaspoon black pepper
- 10 green onions, thinly sliced
- ¾ cup sliced almonds

ONE In a large saucepan bring water and salt to boiling; add noodles. Cook for 3 to 5 minutes or until just tender. Drain well; place in a large bowl.

TWO Meanwhile, for dressing, in a small saucepan preheat vegetable oil and sesame oil. Cook and stir sesame seeds in hot until the seeds are lightly browned. Remove saucepan from heat; stir in soy sauce, coriander, salt, and pepper.

THREE Pour hot dressing over noodles; toss to coat. Add green onion and almonds; toss to combine. Serve warm, at room temperature, or chilled.

PLAN AHEAD: Prepare noodles up to 3 days ahead. Cover and refrigerate.

Fresh Summer Tomato Sauce for Pasta

MAKE THIS SAUCE ALL SUMMER LONG WHILE THE TOMATOES ARE AT THEIR BEST. FREEZE IN BAGS OR CANNING JARS.

SIDES: Spinach with Lemon and Parmesan (page 215) and garlic bread.

DESSERT: Biscotti and ice cream.

MAKES: about 4½ cups (3 to 4 servings)

- 4 large ripe tomatoes, cut into ½-inch pieces, or one 28-ounce can chopped tomatoes, undrained
- 1 cup chopped fresh basil
- ½ cup grated Parmesan cheese
- ½ cup grated onion
- ¼ cup extra-virgin olive oil
- 2 teaspoons minced fresh garlic
- 1 teaspoon dried oregano, crushed
- 1 teaspoon salt
- ½ teaspoon black pepper
  Hot cooked pasta

ONE In a large bowl stir together tomato, basil, Parmesan cheese, onion, oil, garlic, oregano, salt, and pepper. Cover and let stand at room temperature for 1 to 2 hours. Serve over pasta.

Caesar Pasta Salad

WE CONCOCTED THIS RECIPE WHEN WE OWNED A SANDWICH SHOP AT A LOCAL MALL. IT WAS OUR MOST REQUESTED SALAD AND IS HEARTY ENOUGH TO SERVE AS A MAIN DISH.

SIDE: Cheesy Rosemary Polenta (page 173).

DESSERT: No-Bake Chocolate Cookies (page 227).

MAKES: 6 servings

- 12 **ounces dried bow tie pasta (or pasta of your choice)**
- 1 **cup bottled Caesar salad dressing**
- 8 **ounces sliced fresh mushrooms**
- 1 **cup finely shredded Parmesan cheese**
- ½ **cup sliced red bell pepper**
- ½ **cup sliced green Greek olives or sliced, pitted black or green olives**
- ½ **cup sliced green onion**

ONE Cook pasta according to package directions; drain. Place pasta in a large bowl. Pour salad dressing over warm pasta; toss to coat. Add mushrooms, ¾ cup of the Parmesan cheese, bell pepper, olives, and green onion; toss to combine.

TWO Serve immediately, topping with remaining ¼ cup cheese or cover and refrigerate for several hours.

PLAN AHEAD: Up to 3 days ahead cook the pasta; drain, and rinse. Toss with 1 tablespoon olive oil and refrigerate in a resealable plastic bag.

Tortellini with Vegetables

THREE-CHEESE TORTELLINI IS EASY TO FIND EITHER FRESH OR FROZEN.

VEGETARIAN

SIDES: Mixed green salad with Croutons (page 166).

DESSERT: Bread Pudding (page 234).

MAKES: 10 servings

Nonstick cooking spray

2   tablespoons olive oil

8   ounces fresh mushrooms, sliced

1   zucchini, thinly sliced

½   cup finely chopped onion

2   cups fresh or frozen uncooked three-cheese tortellini

4   cups Basic Marinara Sauce (page 38)

1   cup shredded mozzarella cheese

ONE Preheat oven to 350°F. Coat a 13×9×2-inch baking dish with cooking spray.

TWO Preheat oil in large skillet. Saute mushrooms, zucchini, and onion in hot oil until tender. Arrange tortellini in prepared baking dish. Top with cooked vegetables. Pour Basic Marinara Sauce over vegetables.

THREE Bake, uncovered, for 20 minutes. Sprinkle with cheese; bake 10 minutes more.

FREEZE AHEAD: Prepare through Step Two. Cover with plastic wrap and foil. Freeze up to 2 months. Defrost completely in refrigerator. Preheat oven. Remove plastic wrap and foil and continue according to Step Three.

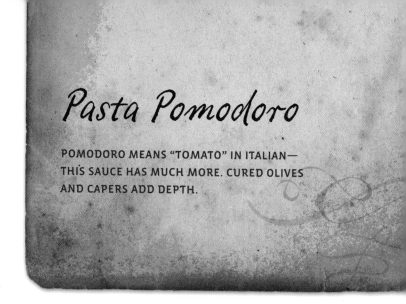

Pasta Pomodoro

POMODORO MEANS "TOMATO" IN ITALIAN—
THIS SAUCE HAS MUCH MORE. CURED OLIVES
AND CAPERS ADD DEPTH.

SIDE: Tomato-Basil Crostini
(page 159).

DESSERT: Fishbowl Trifle (page 248).

MAKES: 6 servings

- ¼ cup olive oil
- 3 cups chopped onion
- 1 tablespoon minced fresh garlic
- 5 cups water
- 2 8-ounce cans tomato paste
- 2 tablespoons grated Parmesan cheese
- 1 tablespoon salt (or to taste)
- 2 teaspoons dried oregano, crushed
- 1 teaspoon dried Italian mixed herbs, crushed
- ½ teaspoon black pepper
- 2 cups dried macaroni
- ½ cup chopped green bell pepper
- 2 cups chopped tomatoes
- ½ cup coarsely chopped oil-cured Greek olives
- ½ cup drained capers

ONE For sauce, preheat 2 tablespoons of the oil in a large saucepan. Saute 2 cups of the onion and the garlic in hot oil until tender. Add water, tomato paste, Parmesan cheese, salt, oregano, Italian herbs, and black pepper. Turn heat to low. Cover and simmer for 2 to 3 hours, stirring often to prevent scorching.

TWO Prepare the pasta according to package directions; drain.

THREE Preheat the remaining 2 tablespoons oil in a large skillet. Saute the remaining 1 cup onion and the bell pepper just until tender. Add to sauce along with cooked macaroni, tomatoes, olives, and capers. Simmer, uncovered, 5 minutes.

FREEZE AHEAD: Prepare through Step One; cool completely. Place in a freezer bag and freeze up to 2 months. Defrost completely in refrigerator. Reheat over low heat.

Hot Orzo Salad

ORZO MEANS "BARLEY" IN ITALIAN AND IS USED TO DESCRIBE RICE-SHAPE PASTA.

SIDE: Toasted pita bread, brushed with olive oil and Parmesan cheese.

DESSERT: Boston Cream Cakes: Prepare one 3-ounce box instant vanilla pudding. Top slices of purchased pound cake with pudding; drizzle with chocolate syrup.

MAKES: 6 servings

- 1 pound dried orzo
- ½ cup olive oil
- ¼ cup freshly squeezed lemon juice
- 1 tablespoon chopped fresh dill
- 2 cloves garlic, minced
- 1 teaspoon salt (or to taste)
- ½ teaspoon black pepper
- 1 cup thinly sliced yellow bell pepper
- 1 cup thinly sliced red bell pepper
- 3 green onions, thinly sliced
- ½ cup kalamata olives, pitted and coarsely chopped
- 1 teaspoon dried Italian mixed herbs, crushed
- 6 ounces feta cheese, crumbled

ONE Cook orzo according to package directions; drain.

TWO Meanwhile, for vinaigrette, in a small bowl whisk together oil, lemon juice, dill, garlic, salt, and black pepper. Set aside.

THREE In a large bowl combine hot cooked orzo, yellow bell pepper, red bell pepper, green onion, olives, and Italian herbs. Pour vinaigrette over orzo mixture; toss to coat. Add feta cheese; toss to combine.

FREEZE AHEAD: Place salad in a freezer bag and freeze up to 2 months. Defrost completely in refrigerator.

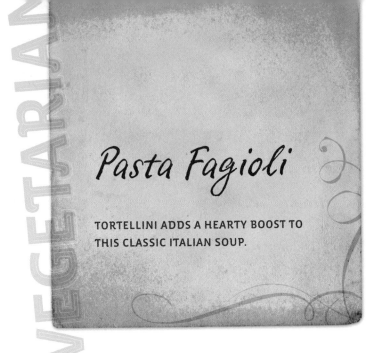

Pasta Fagioli

TORTELLINI ADDS A HEARTY BOOST TO THIS CLASSIC ITALIAN SOUP.

SIDE: Caesar Salad (page 193).

DESSERT: Mixed Berry Ice Cream Shortcakes: Split bakery scones in half. Fill with ice cream; top with frozen mixed berries (thawed) and whipped dessert topping.

MAKES: 6 servings

- 2 tablespoons olive oil
- 1 cup chopped onion
- ½ cup chopped celery
- 1 teaspoon minced fresh garlic
- 1 recipe Basic Marinara Sauce (page 38)
- 4 cups chicken broth or water
- 1 28-ounce can small white beans, undrained
- ½ teaspoon dried rosemary, crushed
- ½ teaspoon dried oregano, crushed
- 3 cups dried uncooked tri-color cheese-filled tortellini

ONE Preheat oil in a 4- to 6-quart Dutch oven or soup pot. Saute onion, celery, and garlic in hot oil until tender. Stir in Basic Marinara Sauce, broth, undrained beans, rosemary, and oregano. Turn heat to low. Cover and simmer 30 minutes.

TWO Meanwhile, cook tortellini according to package directions; drain. Stir into soup just before serving.

FREEZE AHEAD: Prepare through Step One. Place in a freezer bag and freeze up to 2 months. Defrost completely in refrigerator. Reheat over low heat while cooking tortellini.

Corn and Black Bean Salad

THE LAST TIME I MADE THIS, I USED FRESHLY COOKED CORN ON THE COB. IT MADE THE SALAD EVEN MORE DELICIOUS.

SIDE: Green Chile and Cheese Corn Bread (page 164).

DESSERT: Frozen Yogurt Pops (page 230).

MAKES: 8 servings

- 4 cups frozen corn
- 2 15-ounce cans black beans, drained and rinsed
- 4 green onions, thinly sliced
- 1 medium red bell pepper, thinly sliced
- 1 medium green bell pepper, thinly sliced
- 1 4-ounce can diced green chile peppers, undrained
- ½ cup chopped fresh cilantro
- 1 tablespoon chili powder
- 2 teaspoons minced fresh garlic
- 1 teaspoon salt (or to taste)
- ½ teaspoon black pepper
- 1 cup bottled Italian salad dressing

ONE In a large salad bowl toss together corn, black beans, green onion, bell pepper, undrained green chile peppers, cilantro, chili powder, garlic, salt, and black pepper. Pour salad dressing over bean mixture; toss to coat.

TWO Cover and refrigerate at least 1 hour.

FREEZE AHEAD: Place all ingredients in a freezer bag and freeze up to 2 months. Defrost completely in refrigerator.

Spicy Vegetarian Chili

SPICY CANNED TOMATOES LEND A ZESTY TASTE TO THIS CHILI.

SIDE: Endive and Apple Salad (page 194).

DESSERT: Fudge brownies.

MAKES: 4 to 6 servings

- ½ cup wheat berries
- 3 cups water
- 2 tablespoons olive oil
- ½ cup chopped zucchini
- ½ cup chopped onion
- ½ cup chopped bell pepper
- ½ cup chopped celery
- 3 cups canned chopped tomatoes, undrained
- 2 cups canned spicy diced tomatoes and green chiles, undrained
- 1 cup frozen corn
- 1 cup canned pinto beans
- 1 cup canned red beans
- ½ cup canned black beans
- ½ cup canned garbanzo beans
- ½ cup tomato paste
- 2 tablespoons chili powder
- 1 tablespoon salt
- ½ teaspoon black pepper
- 1 to 2 cups water

ONE In a bowl soak wheat berries, covered, in the 3 cups water in the refrigerator overnight. Drain wheat berries.

TWO Preheat oil in a large soup pot. Saute zucchini, onion, bell pepper, and celery in hot oil until tender. Add soaked and drained wheat berries, undrained tomatoes, undrained tomatoes and green chiles, corn, pinto beans, red beans, black beans, garbanzo beans, tomato paste, chili powder, salt, and black pepper. Add the 1 to 2 cups water, depending on the consistency you want.

THREE Cover and simmer about 20 minutes or until heated through.

FREEZE AHEAD: Combine soaked and drained wheat berries and the remaining ingredients (except the 1 to 2 cups water) in a freezer bag and freeze up to 2 months. Defrost completely in refrigerator. Place in a soup pot and add water. Continue according to Step Three.

Red Beans and Rice

SAUTEED "TRINITY" (ONIONS, CELERY, BELL PEPPER)
AND CREOLE SEASONING MAKE THESE BEANS TASTE
LIKE THEY WERE SIMMERED ALL DAY.

VEGETARIAN

SIDE: Corn bread.

DESSERT: Miracle Pecan-Caramel
Bars (page 226).

MAKES: 6 servings

- 2½ cups water
- 1 cup uncooked long grain white rice
- 1 teaspoon salt
- 2 tablespoons olive oil
- ½ cup finely chopped onion
- ½ cup chopped celery
- ¼ cup chopped bell pepper
- 1 teaspoon minced fresh garlic
- 2 16-ounce cans red beans, undrained
- 1 12-ounce can crushed tomatoes, undrained
- 1 teaspoon Creole seasoning

ONE In a saucepan combine water, rice, and salt. Bring to boiling over medium-high heat. Turn heat to low. Cover and simmer 20 minutes.

TWO Meanwhile, preheat oil in a large skillet. Saute onion, celery, bell pepper, and garlic in hot oil until tender. Stir in undrained beans, undrained tomatoes, and Creole seasoning; simmer, uncovered, for 15 minutes.

THREE Serve bean mixture over rice.

FREEZE AHEAD: Prepare beans (Step Two). Place in a freezer bag and freeze up to 2 months. Defrost completely in refrigerator. Reheat over low heat while cooking rice (Step One). Continue according to Step Three.

Sour Cream Veggie Enchiladas with Salsa Verde

TOMATILLOS AND GREEN CHILES MAKE AN INTERESTING SAUCE THAT IS PERFECT WITH THE VEGETABLE FILLING.

SIDES: Shredded iceberg lettuce, guacamole, and chopped tomatoes.

DESSERT: Strawberry Ice Cream Pie: Spread softened strawberry ice cream over one 9-inch cookie crumb piecrust. Freeze until firm.

MAKES: 12 enchiladas

- 1 to 2 cups vegetable oil
- 12 6-inch corn tortillas
- 2 tablespoons olive oil
- 2 cups diced zucchini
- 1 cup diced fresh mushrooms
- 4 cups shredded Monterey Jack cheese
- 1 cup frozen corn
- 1 cup canned black beans, drained and rinsed
- 1 cup thinly sliced green onion
- 1 recipe Salsa Verde
- 2 cups sour cream

ONE In a medium skillet preheat ½ inch vegetable oil over medium heat. Use tongs to immerse tortillas, one at a time, into hot oil. Cook tortillas only a few seconds (just enough to soften; don't let them crisp on the edges). Drain tortillas on paper towels.

TWO Preheat oven to 375°F. Preheat olive oil in a large skillet. Saute zucchini and mushrooms in hot olive oil until tender. Remove skillet from heat. Stir in 2 cups of the cheese, corn, black beans, and green onion.

THREE Spread about ¾ cup of the Salsa Verde in the bottom of a 13×9×2-inch baking dish. Use tongs to dip one fried tortilla in some of the remaining Salsa Verde. Top tortilla with some of the vegetable mixture. Roll up tortilla. Place, seam side down, in baking dish. Repeat with remaining tortillas and vegetable mixture. Spoon remaining Salsa Verde over enchiladas. Sprinkle with the remaining 2 cups cheese.

FOUR Bake, uncovered, for 20 to 25 minutes or until hot and bubbly. Spread sour cream evenly over enchiladas. Serve immediately.

SALSA VERDE: Peel 1 pound fresh tomatillos; cut in half. Place tomatillos in a large saucepan. Cover with water; simmer until very tender. Drain; cool slightly. Place tomatillos in a blender along with 1 cup chopped onion, 1 cup chicken broth, 2 tablespoons minced fresh garlic, and 1 tablespoon salt. Blend until smooth. Add three 7-ounce cans diced green chile peppers, undrained, and enough additional chicken broth to make about 4 cups sauce; blend to desired smoothness. Preheat 2 tablespoons olive oil in a large skillet over medium heat. Transfer tomatillo mixture to skillet. Turn heat to low. Cook, stirring occasionally, for 10 minutes.

Greek Pitas

BE AS CREATIVE AS YOU WISH, ADDING OTHER VEGETABLES OR TOFU.

SIDE: Simple Tortellini Salad (page 192).

DESSERT: Cream Cheese Pie (page 241).

MAKES: 8 sandwiches

- 8 ounces crumbled feta cheese
- 2 medium tomatoes, diced
- 1 large cucumber, peeled and diced
- 1 small red onion, thinly sliced
- ¼ cup sliced, pitted black olives
- 3 tablespoons olive oil
- 3 tablespoons freshly squeezed lemon juice
- 1 teaspoon dried oregano, crushed
- 1 teaspoon salt
- ½ teaspoon black pepper
- 8 lettuce leaves
- 4 pita bread rounds, halved
- ½ cup alfalfa sprouts

ONE In large bowl combine feta cheese, tomato, cucumber, onion, and olives. For dressing, in a small bowl combine oil, lemon juice, oregano, salt, and pepper. Pour dressing over vegetable mixture; toss to coat.

TWO Place 1 lettuce leaf inside each pita bread pocket; fill with vegetable mixture. Top with alfalfa sprouts.

PLAN AHEAD: Prepare dressing up to 1 week ahead. Cover and refrigerate. Keep pita bread frozen up to 1 month.

Rio Grande Skillet

TRUST ME—THIS RECIPE WILL GET YOU OUT OF MANY LAST-MINUTE DINNER DILEMMAS. EAT THIS MEXICAN-STYLE DISH FOR DINNER OR AS A DIP WITH CORN CHIPS.

SIDE: Steamed Broccoli Salad with Pine Nuts and Raisins (page 180).

DESSERT: Chocolate ice cream sandwiched between peanut butter cookies.

MAKES: 6 to 8 servings

- 1 16-ounce can refried beans
- 1 16-ounce can black beans, drained and rinsed
- 2 cups shredded cheddar cheese
- 1 cup sour cream
- 2 tablespoons taco seasoning mix
- 1 cup prepared guacamole
- 1 cup shredded iceberg lettuce
- 1 medium tomato, chopped
- ½ cup chopped green onion
- ½ cup salsa

  Corn chips

ONE In a 12-inch skillet cook refried beans and black beans over medium heat until hot. Top with cheese. Cover and heat for 1 to 2 minutes or until cheese melts. Remove skillet from heat.

TWO In a small bowl stir together sour cream and taco seasoning mix; spread over melted cheese. Top with guacamole, lettuce, tomato, green onion, and salsa. Serve immediately with corn chips.

Santa Fe Strata

CREATE A STRATA FOR BREAKFAST, LUNCH, OR DINNER. IT'S PERFECT FOR A FANCY BRUNCH.

SIDE: Fresh fruit salad.

DESSERT: Sweet Brown Bread Sandwiches: Brown bread comes in a can in the baking section of the grocery store. Slice the bread and spread with softened cream cheese to make little round sandwiches.

MAKES: 12 servings

Nonstick cooking spray

- 2 tablespoons olive oil
- 2 cups sliced fresh mushrooms
- ½ cup chopped onion
- 6 7-inch flour tortillas
- 4 cups shredded Monterey Jack cheese
- ½ cup canned diced green chile peppers, undrained
- 1 cup frozen corn
- ½ cup chopped fresh cilantro
- 6 eggs
- 2 cups milk
- 1 teaspoon minced fresh garlic
- ¼ teaspoon black pepper

ONE Preheat oven to 350°F. Coat a 13×9×2-inch baking dish with cooking spray.

TWO In a skillet saute mushrooms and onion in hot oil until tender.

THREE Line prepared dish with tortillas, tearing to fit. Layer mushroom mixture, cheese, undrained chile peppers, corn, and cilantro over tortillas. In a large bowl beat together eggs, milk, garlic, and black pepper; pour over layers in dish.

FOUR Bake, uncovered, for 45 to 55 minutes or until a knife inserted in center of dish comes out clean. Let stand 10 minutes before serving.

FREEZE AHEAD: Prepare through Step Three. Cover with plastic wrap and foil. Freeze up to 2 months. Defrost completely in refrigerator. Preheat oven. Remove plastic wrap and foil and continue according to Step Four.

Charro Bean Soft Tacos

THE BEANS IN THIS RECIPE ARE SO GOOD YOU CAN EAT THEM SERVED OVER TORTILLA CHIPS OR AS A SIDE DISH.

SIDES: Yellow rice or Chef Duane's Spanish Rice (page 158), shredded iceberg lettuce and chopped tomatoes tossed with salsa.

DESSERT: Mango Sundaes: Top scoops of vanilla ice cream with sliced mangoes and shredded coconut.

MAKES: 6 servings

- 1 tablespoon olive oil
- ½ cup chopped onion
- 1 clove garlic, minced
- 1 16-ounce can pinto beans, undrained
- 1 16-ounce can refried beans
- 1 14½-ounce can diced tomatoes, undrained
- 1 teaspoon chili powder
- ½ teaspoon salt
- ¼ teaspoon black pepper
- 2 tablespoons chopped fresh cilantro
- 12 6-inch flour tortillas

ONE Preheat oil in a large skillet. Saute onion and garlic in hot oil until tender. Stir in undrained pinto beans, refried beans, undrained tomatoes, chili powder, salt, and pepper.

TWO Simmer, stirring constantly, for 1 minute (if more liquid is needed, add water or vegetable broth). Stir in cilantro.

THREE Serve bean mixture in tortillas.

FREEZE AHEAD: Prepare through Step One. Place in a freezer container and freeze up to 2 months. Defrost completely in refrigerator. Continue according to Step Two.

Cowboy Caviar

SERVE THIS FUN MIX IN TORTILLAS, WITH TORTILLA CHIPS, OVER TOSSED SALAD, OR IN A BOWL ALL BY ITSELF.

SIDE: Sliced fresh fruit.

DESSERT: Frozen Adobe Pie (page 239).

MAKES: 6 to 8 servings

- 1 16-ounce can black-eyed peas, drained
- 1 16-ounce can black beans, drained and rinsed
- 1 16-ounce can garbanzo beans, drained
- 1 cup thinly sliced green onion
- 1 7-ounce can diced green chile peppers, undrained
- ½ cup finely chopped red bell pepper
- ½ cup finely chopped green bell pepper
- ½ cup chopped fresh cilantro
- ¼ cup sliced pickled jalapeño chile peppers (or to taste) (optional)
- 2 teaspoons minced fresh garlic
- 1 cup picante sauce or salsa
- ½ cup bottled Italian salad dressing
- 1 teaspoon salt (or to taste)
- ½ teaspoon black pepper
- 12 6-inch flour tortillas

ONE In a large bowl combine black-eyed peas, black beans, garbanzo beans, green onion, undrained green chile peppers, red bell pepper, green bell pepper, cilantro, pickled jalapeño peppers (if desired), and garlic.

TWO Add picante sauce, salad dressing, salt, and black pepper; toss to combine. Serve immediately or cover and refrigerate. Serve with tortillas.

FREEZE AHEAD: Place all ingredients, except tortillas, in a freezer bag and freeze up to 2 months. Defrost completely in refrigerator.

Stuffed Veggie Pizza

TWO LAYERS OF TENDER PIZZA CRUST ARE FILLED WITH YOUR FAMILY'S FAVORITE TOPPINGS.

SIDE: Asparagus Baked with Cheese (page 220).

DESSERT: Granola Ice Cream: Top ice cream with your favorite granola.

MAKES: 8 to 10 servings

Nonstick cooking spray

- 1 loaf frozen bread dough, thawed
- 1 cup pizza sauce
- 1 14¾-ounce can artichoke hearts, drained and chopped
- 1 cup canned mushrooms, drained
- ½ cup chopped sun-dried tomatoes
- ½ cup chopped onion
- ½ cup chopped bell pepper
- 1 cup shredded mozzarella cheese
- 2 tablespoons olive oil
- 1 teaspoon kosher salt

ONE Preheat oven to 350°F. Coat a 13×9×2-inch baking dish with cooking spray.

TWO Cut bread dough in half; roll out one half to fit inside the bottom of the prepared baking dish. Spread pizza sauce over dough. Top with artichokes, mushrooms, tomatoes, onion, and bell pepper. Sprinkle with cheese. Roll out remaining dough half to fit over the top of the pizza. Brush dough with oil; sprinkle with salt.

THREE Bake, uncovered, about 30 minutes or until crust is golden brown. Let stand 5 minutes before serving.

FREEZE AHEAD: Prepare through Step Two. Cover with plastic wrap and foil. Freeze up to 2 months. Defrost completely in refrigerator. Let stand 30 to 60 minutes at room temperature before baking. Preheat oven. Remove plastic wrap and foil and continue according to Step Three.

Bruschetta with Cannellini Salad

BRUSCHETTA IS GREAT FOR BUNCH, LUNCH, SUPPER, OR AS AN HORS D'OEUVRE. THE BEAN MIXTURE IS ALSO DELICIOUS BY ITSELF AS A SALAD.

VEGETARIAN

SIDE: Caesar Salad (page 193).

DESSERT: Caramel Pears: Drizzle drained canned pear slices with caramel sauce.

MAKES: 4 to 8 servings

- 3 cups Italian Bean Topping (page 168) or two 14½-ounce cans cannellini beans, drained and rinsed
- ½ cup olive oil
- ½ cup balsamic vinegar
- ½ cup finely chopped yellow or red bell pepper
- ½ cup finely chopped onion
- ¼ cup chopped sun-dried tomatoes
- ¼ cup fresh basil, cut in chiffonade
- 2 cloves garlic, minced
- 1 teaspoon salt (or to taste)
- ½ teaspoon black pepper (or to taste)
- 8 ½-inch slices dense Italian bread, toasted or grilled

ONE In a large bowl toss together Italian Bean Topping or canned beans, oil, vinegar, bell pepper, onion, tomatoes, basil, garlic, salt, and black pepper. Cover and refrigerate for 1 hour.

TWO Serve on top of toasted bread slices.

FREEZE AHEAD: Combine all ingredients except basil. Place in a freezer bag and freeze up to 2 months. Defrost completely in refrigerator. Add basil. Continue according to Step Two. (If mixture is watery, drain before using.)

bread, grain & rice

Pecan Wild Rice Pilaf

THIS PILAF IS FANCY ENOUGH FOR A DINNER PARTY, YET SIMPLE TO MAKE.

MAKES: 8 servings

4½	cups chicken broth
1	cup uncooked wild rice
3	tablespoons butter
1	cup uncooked regular brown rice
2	shallots, minced
½	cup sliced fresh mushrooms
½	cup coarsely chopped pecans
¼	cup chopped fresh parsley
1	teaspoon salt
¼	teaspoon black pepper

ONE In a saucepan combine 2 cups of the chicken broth, wild rice, and 1 tablespoon of the butter. Bring to boiling over high heat. Turn heat to low. Cook, covered, about 1 hour or until liquid is absorbed and rice is tender.

TWO Meanwhile, in another saucepan combine the remaining 2½ cups broth, brown rice, and 1 tablespoon of the butter. Bring to boiling over high heat. Turn heat to low. Cook, covered, about 50 minutes or until liquid is absorbed and rice is tender.

THREE Meanwhile, melt the remaining 1 tablespoon butter in a medium skillet over medium heat. Cook and stir shallot and mushrooms in hot butter for 5 minutes.

FOUR In a large bowl toss together cooked wild rice, cooked brown rice, mushroom mixture, pecans, parsley, salt, and pepper. Serve immediately.

PLAN AHEAD: Prepare pilaf up to 1 day ahead. Cover and refrigerate. To reheat, preheat oven to 350°F. Place pilaf in a casserole. Bake, covered, about 20 minutes or until hot.

Lemon Parmesan Risotto

PARMESAN ADDS EVEN MORE CREAMY CONSISTENCY TO THIS RISOTTO, AND LEMON GIVES IT A NICE TANG.

MAKES: 8 servings

- 2 tablespoons butter
- 2 tablespoons olive oil
- ½ cup finely chopped onion
- 2 tablespoons lemon zest
- 3 cups uncooked Arborio rice
- 1 cup dry white wine
- 9 cups unsalted chicken broth
- 1 cup freshly grated Parmesan cheese
- 2 tablespoons freshly squeezed lemon juice
- 1 teaspoon salt (or to taste)
- ¼ teaspoon black pepper (or to taste)

ONE Melt 1 tablespoon of the butter with the oil in a large saucepan over medium heat. Add onion and lemon zest; cook and stir for 2 to 3 minutes. Add uncooked rice. Cook and stir about 1 minute or until rice gives off a nutty fragrance. Carefully add wine. Turn heat to medium-low. Cook and stir until wine is absorbed.

TWO Add ½ cup broth, cooking and stirring constantly until absorbed. Repeat adding broth, ½ cup at a time, until all the broth is used. Add the remaining 1 tablespoon butter, Parmesan cheese, and lemon juice, stirring until butter melts. Stir in salt and pepper. Serve immediately.

Fried Rice

TURN THIS RICE INTO A GREAT ENTRÉE BY ADDING 1 TO 2 CUPS COOKED MEAT OR TOFU.

MAKES: 4 servings

¼ cup vegetable oil

3 eggs, beaten

4 cups cooked long grain white rice

5 green onions, chopped

2 cloves garlic, minced

½ cup frozen peas and carrot mix

¼ cup chopped fresh parsley

2 tablespoons toasted sesame oil

1 tablespoon soy sauce

1 teaspoon salt (or to taste)

½ teaspoon black pepper (or to taste)

ONE Preheat 1 tablespoon of the vegetable oil in a wok or large skillet. Add eggs; scramble eggs. Transfer eggs to a plate; set aside.

TWO Add the remaining 3 tablespoons vegetable oil to hot wok; add cooked rice. Cook and stir until golden and hot. Add green onion and garlic; cook and stir for 1 minute. Add peas and carrot mix, parsley, sesame oil, and soy sauce. Cook and stir about 2 minutes or until peas are bright green and hot. Stir in scrambled eggs, salt, and pepper; heat through.

PLAN AHEAD: When cooking rice for another meal, make extra to use in this recipe.

Chef Duane's Spanish Rice

THIS IS CHEF DUANE'S VERSION OF AUTHENTIC SPANISH RICE. HIS SECRET INGREDIENT IS THE TOMATO-FLAVORED BOUILLON CUBE.

RICE

MAKES: 6 to 8 servings

- 2 cups uncooked long grain white rice
- 3 cups chicken stock
- 1 tomato-flavored bouillon cube
- 2 tablespoons vegetable oil
- 1 cup chopped onion
- 2 teaspoons minced garlic
- 1 teaspoon ground cumin
- 2 teaspoons chili powder
- 1 tablespoon salt
- ½ teaspoon black pepper

ONE Place rice in a strainer; rinse well with cold water. Set aside.

TWO In a small saucepan heat chicken stock and bouillon cube until the cube dissolves. Set aside.

THREE In a large saucepan heat vegetable oil. Saute onion and garlic until tender. Add rice to the pan and saute until translucent. Stir in cumin, chili powder, salt, pepper, and chicken stock mixture. Bring to a boil; cover and simmer 20 minutes. Turn off heat; uncover rice and fluff with a fork.

TIP: Rinsing the uncooked rice is the secret to fluffy rice. It washes off the sticky starch layer.

NOTE: You can find tomato bouillon cubes in Asian, Hispanic, and gourmet grocery stores. If it is not available in your area, you can substitute 1 chicken bouillon cube and 1 tablespoon of tomato paste for the tomato-flavored bouillon cube.

Tomato-Basil Crostini

CROSTINI IS GREAT AS A SIDE WITH PASTA DISHES. IT CAN STAND AS AN ENTRÉE IF YOU ALLOW FOR LARGER SERVINGS AND ADD A FEW HEARTY INGREDIENTS—SEE OPTIONS, BELOW.

MAKES: 4 servings

- 2 ripe tomatoes, seeded and finely chopped
- ¼ cup olive oil
- 1 tablespoon balsamic vinegar
- 4 to 6 fresh basil leaves, finely chopped
- 1 teaspoon minced fresh garlic
- ½ teaspoon salt
- ¼ teaspoon black pepper
- 4 ½-inch slices French or Italian bread

ONE In a bowl stir together tomato, 2 tablespoons of the oil, vinegar, basil, garlic, salt, and pepper. Cover and refrigerate for 30 to 60 minutes.

TWO Preheat broiler. Arrange bread slices on broiler pan. Brush both sides of each bread slice with some of the remaining 2 tablespoons oil. Broil 2 to 4 minutes or until golden brown, turning once.

THREE To serve, spoon some of the tomato mixture on top of each toasted bread slice.

OPTIONS: Add any of the following to the tomato mixture: chopped pepperoni or other cooked Italian sausage, chopped cooked chicken or ham, cubed cheese or tofu.

Cinnamon Pull-Apart Bread

FOR AS LONG AS THEY CAN REMEMBER, MY KIDS HAVE EATEN THIS ON CHRISTMAS MORNING. JUST THE SMELL OF IT BAKING REMINDS THEM OF CHILDHOOD HOLIDAYS.

MAKES: 12 to 14 servings

- 3 10-ounce cans refrigerated flaky biscuits
- 1 cup butter
- 1½ cups packed brown sugar
- 1 cup chopped pecans (optional)
- 1 tablespoon ground cinnamon

ONE Preheat oven to 350°F. Remove biscuits from cans and cut into quarters. (Cutting the biscuits into quarters is easy if you take a third of a roll at a time, lay it on its side, and use a serrated knife to slice in half and then in half again to make quarters.)

TWO In a saucepan melt butter; stir in brown sugar, pecans (if desired), and cinnamon, stirring until brown sugar dissolves..

THREE Place half the biscuits in the bottom of a fluted tube pan; drizzle with half of the melted butter mixture. Add remaining biscuits; drizzle with the remaining melted butter mixture.

FOUR Bake, uncovered, for 35 minutes. Let stand for 5 minutes before turning out onto a serving platter.

Stuffed Greek Bread

TRY THIS GREAT COMBINATION OF MEDITERRANEAN
FLAVORS AND CRUSTY BREAD.

MAKES: 8 pieces

- 1 loaf French bread
- 2 cups shredded mozzarella cheese
- ½ cup mayonnaise
- ½ cup butter, softened
- 6 green onions, chopped
- ¼ cup finely chopped Greek black olives
- 1 tablespoon chopped capers
- 1 teaspoon minced fresh garlic

ONE Preheat oven to 350°F. Cut bread in half lengthwise; cut each half crosswise into 4 pieces. In a bowl stir together cheese, mayonnaise, butter, green onions, olives, capers, and garlic. Spread cheese mixture over top of bread pieces.

TWO Arrange bread pieces on a large baking sheet. Bake for 10 to 12 minutes or until heated through.

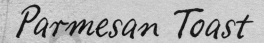

Parmesan Toast

THIN, CRISPY TOASTS WITH MELTED PARMESAN CHEESE, THESE ADD CRUNCH TO SALADS, SOUPS, OR ANY MEAL.

MAKES: 4 to 6 servings

12 ¼-inch slices baguette-style French bread

¼ cup olive oil

¾ to 1½ cups shredded Parmesan cheese

ONE Preheat broiler. Place bread slices on a baking sheet. Brush each bread slice with olive oil. Broil until toasted.

TWO Sprinkle each piece of toast with 1 to 2 tablespoons Parmesan cheese. Broil until cheese melts and begins to brown.

PLAN AHEAD: Prepare through Step Two up to 1 week ahead. Store at room temperature in an airtight container.

FREEZE AHEAD: Prepare through Step Two. Place toast in a freezer bag and freeze up to 2 months.

Green Chile and Cheese Corn Bread

MOIST, CHEESY, AND FILLING—THIS IS COMFORT-FOOD BREAD.

MAKES: 6 to 8 servings

Nonstick cooking spray

- 1 cup cornmeal
- 1 teaspoon salt
- ½ teaspoon baking soda
- 1 17-ounce can creamed corn
- 1½ cups shredded cheddar cheese
- ½ cup finely chopped onion
- ¼ cup vegetable oil
- 2 eggs, beaten
- 1 4-ounce can diced green chile peppers, undrained

ONE Preheat oven to 375°F. Coat an 8-inch baking dish with cooking spray.

TWO In a large bowl stir together cornmeal, salt, and baking soda. Stir in creamed corn, cheese, onion, oil, eggs, and undrained chile peppers.

THREE Pour batter into prepared baking dish. Bake for 45 minutes.

FREEZE AHEAD: Place baked corn bread in a freezer bag and freeze up to 2 months.

Croutons

THESE FRESHLY BAKED CROUTONS ARE SURE TO SPOIL YOU.

MAKES: 4 to 6 cups

- ½ loaf French bread
- ¼ cup olive oil
- 1 teaspoon minced fresh garlic
- ½ teaspoon dried Italian mixed herbs, crushed

ONE Preheat oven to 375°F. Use a serrated knife to cut bread into ½-inch cubes. Place cubes in a large bowl.

TWO In a small saucepan heat olive oil, garlic, and Italian herbs until garlic gives off an aroma. Drizzle oil mixture over bread cubes; toss to coat.

THREE Spread bread cubes in a single layer on a baking sheet. Bake for 10 to 15 minutes or until crisp and golden, stirring once.

PLAN AHEAD: Prepare Croutons up to 1 week ahead. Store at room temperature in an airtight container.

FREEZE AHEAD: Place Croutons in a freezer bag and freeze up to 2 months.

Corn Bread Dressing

FRITOS® ADD A DEEP, ROASTED CORN FLAVOR
TO THE DRESSING.

MAKES: 8 to 10 servings

Nonstick cooking spray

¼ cup butter

3 stalks celery, diced

2 medium onions, finely chopped

6 cups crumbled corn bread

3 cups chicken or turkey broth

1 cup crushed Fritos®

1 cup dry herb-flavored stuffing mix

2 teaspoons dried sage, crushed

2 teaspoons dried thyme, crushed

1 teaspoon salt (or to taste)

1 teaspoon black pepper (or to taste)

ONE Preheat oven to 350°F. Coat a 2-quart baking dish with cooking spray.

TWO Melt butter in a large skillet. Add celery and onion; cook and stir until tender. Remove skillet from heat. Stir in corn bread, broth, Fritos®, stuffing mix, sage, thyme, salt, and pepper. Spoon dressing into prepared baking dish.

THREE Bake, uncovered, for 45 to 60 minutes or until heated through.

PLAN AHEAD: Prepare through Step Two up to 1 day ahead. Cover and refrigerate. Preheat oven. Uncover and continue according to Step Three.

FREEZE AHEAD: Prepare through Step Two. Cover with plastic wrap and foil. Freeze up to 2 months. Defrost completely in refrigerator. Preheat oven. Remove plastic wrap and foil and continue according to Step Three.

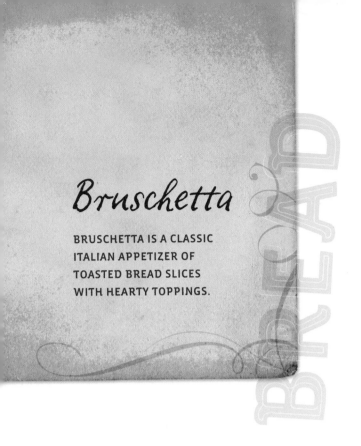

Bruschetta

BRUSCHETTA IS A CLASSIC ITALIAN APPETIZER OF TOASTED BREAD SLICES WITH HEARTY TOPPINGS.

MAKES: 4 to 8 servings

8   ½-inch slices sourdough or country-style bread

2   tablespoons olive oil

Tomato slices

1   recipe Italian Bean Topping

ONE Preheat broiler. Arrange bread slices on a broiler pan. Brush both sides of each bread slice with some of the oil. Broil 2 to 4 minutes or until golden brown, turning once.

TWO To serve, place a couple of halved tomato slices on top of bread slices. Spoon some of the Italian Bean Topping on top of each toasted bread slice.

ITALIAN BEAN TOPPING: In a bowl stir together one 15-ounce can cannellini beans, drained and rinsed; 1 tablespoon olive oil; 1 tablespoon balsamic vinegar; 4 to 6 fresh basil leaves, finely chopped; 1 to 2 teaspoons minced fresh garlic; 1 teaspoon salt; ½ teaspoon dried Italian mixed herbs, crushed; and ½ teaspoon black pepper.

Cheesy Biscuits

A LITTLE EXTRA BAKING POWDER GIVES
THE SELF-RISING FLOUR ADDED STRENGTH
TO HANDLE THE HEAVY CHEESE. THESE
MAKE GREAT HAM OR TURKEY SANDWICHES.

MAKES: 12 biscuits

Nonstick cooking spray

2 cups self-rising flour (do not use all-purpose flour)

1 teaspoon baking powder

¼ cup butter, chilled

¾ cup shredded cheddar cheese

1 cup buttermilk

2 tablespoons butter, melted

ONE Preheat oven to 375°F. Coat a baking sheet with cooking spray.

TWO In a medium bowl combine flour and baking powder. Use a pastry blender or fork to cut in the chilled ¼ cup butter until it resembles cornmeal. Add cheese; toss to coat. Stir in buttermilk until combined.

THREE Transfer dough to a floured surface. Pat dough into a ½-inch-thick circle. Use a 2½-inch biscuit cutter to cut out biscuits.

FOUR Place biscuits on the prepared baking sheet. Brush tops with the 2 tablespoons melted butter. Bake for 8 to 12 minutes or until golden brown

FREEZE AHEAD: Place baked biscuits in a freezer bag and freeze up to 2 months.

Apple and Sausage Stuffing

SALTY SAUSAGE AND SWEET APPLES COMBINE TO CREATE AN INTERESTING FLAVOR.

MAKES: 8 to 10 servings

Nonstick cooking spray

- 1 pound bulk pork sausage
- 1 cup chopped onion
- 1 cup chopped celery
- 6 cups soft white bread crumbs
- 4 large cooking apples, chopped
- 2 cups chopped pecans
- ½ cup chopped fresh parsley
- 2 teaspoons dried sage, crushed
- 2 teaspoons dried thyme, crushed
- 2 teaspoons salt (or to taste)
- 1 teaspoon black pepper
- 2 eggs, slightly beaten
- ½ cup apple juice

ONE Preheat oven to 350°F. Coat a 2-quart baking dish with cooking spray.

TWO In a large skillet cook and crumble sausage until no longer pink; drain on paper towels. Drain fat from skillet but do not wash skillet. Add onion and celery to skillet; cook and stir until tender. Remove skillet from heat. Stir in bread crumbs, apple, pecans, parsley, sage, thyme, salt, and pepper. Add eggs and apple juice; toss to combine. Spoon stuffing into prepared baking dish.

THREE Bake, uncovered, about 1 hour or until heated through, drizzling with additional apple juice as needed if mixture becomes too dry.

PLAN AHEAD: Prepare through Step Two up to 1 day ahead. Cover and refrigerate. Preheat oven. Uncover and continue according to Step Three.

FREEZE AHEAD: Prepare through Step Two. Cover with plastic wrap and foil. Freeze up to 2 months. Defrost completely in refrigerator. Preheat oven. Remove plastic wrap and foil and continue according to Step Three.

Beer Bread

THIS BREAD IS SERVED FOR MOST EVENTS AT THE COOKING SCHOOL. IT ALWAYS GETS CHEERS. BEER SUPPLIES A RUSTIC, EARTHY, YEASTY FLAVOR TO THIS NO-FAIL BREAD.

MAKES: 1 loaf (8 to 10 servings)

Nonstick cooking spray

3 cups self-rising flour (do not use all-purpose flour)

1 12-ounce can beer*

3 tablespoons sugar

3 tablespoons butter, melted or olive oil

ONE Preheat oven to 350°F. Coat an 8×4×2-inch loaf pan with cooking spray.

TWO In a medium bowl, stir together flour, beer, and sugar. (Batter will be like stiff oatmeal.) Spread batter in prepared pan. Bake for 20 minutes. Drizzle top with melted butter; bake 20 minutes more.

THREE Let stand on a wire rack for 10 minutes. Remove from pan; slice.

*NOTE: Any beer will work. Darker ales will produce a stronger-flavored bread.

FREEZE AHEAD: Place baked bread in a freezer bag and freeze up to 2 months.

Cheesy Rosemary Polenta

WHEN I WAS GROWING UP, THERE ALWAYS SEEMED TO BE A LOAF PAN OF GRITS IN THE REFRIGERATOR, JUST WAITING TO BE SLICED AND FRIED. TODAY, THIS DISH IS CALLED BY A MORE SOPHISTICATED NAME, POLENTA, AND WE ADD ALL KINDS OF INTERESTING AND SOMETIMES EXOTIC INGREDIENTS. WITH SLICED MUSHROOMS OR CHOPPED COOKED MEAT, IT EASILY SERVES AS A MAIN DISH.

MAKES: 10 to 12 slices

Nonstick cooking spray

3½ cups water

½ teaspoon salt

1 cup cornmeal

1 cup shredded mozzarella cheese

¼ cup grated Parmesan cheese

2 tablespoons butter

1 teaspoon chopped fresh rosemary

Olive oil

ONE Coat an 8×4×2-inch loaf pan with cooking spray.

TWO In a medium saucepan bring water and salt to boiling. With water boiling, slowly sprinkle in cornmeal, whisking constantly. Cook, whisking constantly, for 5 to 7 minutes or until cornmeal cooks and begins to pull away from the sides of the pan. Whisk in mozzarella cheese, Parmesan cheese, butter, and rosemary. If desired, serve polenta immediately.

THREE Or pour polenta into prepared loaf pan, smoothing the top. Cover and refrigerate until cold. Broil or fry polenta as directed below.

BROILED POLENTA: Preheat broiler. Remove polenta from pan and slice. Lightly brush both sides of polenta with olive oil. Place slices on a large baking sheet. Broil until browned, turning once.

FRIED POLENTA: Remove polenta from pan and slice. Melt 1 tablespoon butter with 1 tablespoon olive oil in a large skillet over medium-high heat. Add polenta slices to skillet. Fry until brown and crispy, turning once.

FREEZE AHEAD: Prepare through Step Two, pouring polenta into loaf pan. Place loaf pan inside a freezer bag and freeze up to 2 months. Defrost completely in refrigerator. Broil or fry as desired.

Fruit and Nut Couscous

SWEET FRUIT, ONIONS, AND ALMONDS CREATE A LOVELY
CONSISTENCY AND DELICIOUS FLAVOR.

MAKES: 4 servings

- 1 cup couscous
- 1½ cups hot water
- ½ cup thinly sliced green onion
- ¼ cup chopped dried apricots
- ¼ cup dried cranberries
- ¼ cup finely chopped fresh cilantro
- ¼ cup sliced almonds
- 2 tablespoons golden raisins
- ¼ cup olive oil
- ¼ cup freshly squeezed lemon juice
- 1 teaspoon salt (or to taste)
- ½ teaspoon black pepper (or to taste)

ONE Place couscous in a large bowl. Use a fork to stir in the hot water. Cover and let stand about 10 minutes or until water is absorbed. Stir in green onion, apricots, cranberries, cilantro, 3 tablespoons of the almonds, and raisins.

TWO In a small bowl whisk together olive oil, lemon juice, salt, and pepper. Pour over couscous; toss to combine. Serve immediately, topping with remaining 1 tablespoon almonds, or cover and refrigerate.

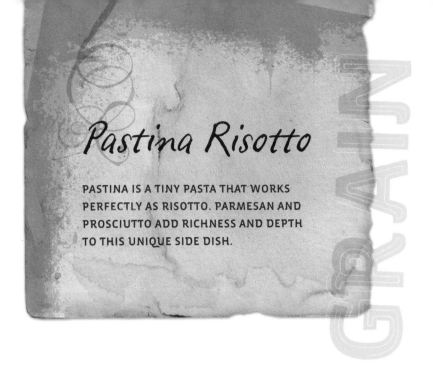

Pastina Risotto

PASTINA IS A TINY PASTA THAT WORKS
PERFECTLY AS RISOTTO. PARMESAN AND
PROSCIUTTO ADD RICHNESS AND DEPTH
TO THIS UNIQUE SIDE DISH.

MAKES: 4 to 6 servings

- 4 cups chicken broth
- ¾ cup chopped onion
- 1 tablespoon minced fresh garlic
- 2 tablespoons olive oil
- 12 ounces dried pastina (such as acini de pepe or any tiny pasta)
- 1½ cups frozen peas
- 1 teaspoon salt
- ½ teaspoon black pepper
- ¾ cup grated Parmesan cheese
- ¼ cup finely chopped prosciutto
- 1 tablespoon butter
- 1½ teaspoons dried oregano, crushed
- 1½ teaspoons dried thyme, crushed

ONE Heat chicken broth in a saucepan; keep warm. In a large saucepan cook and stir onion and garlic in hot oil until tender. Stir in pastina. Add 1 cup of the hot broth to the pastina mixture. Bring to simmering. Cook, stirring constantly, maintaining a slow simmer so pastina doesn't stick. When broth is absorbed, add more, 1 cup at a time, until pastina is almost tender.

TWO Stir in any remaining broth, peas, salt, and pepper. Cook and stir about 3 minutes or until peas and pastina are tender. Remove saucepan from heat. Stir in Parmesan cheese, prosciutto, butter, oregano, and thyme. Serve immediately.

cider vinegar

salads

Sesame Chop Chop Salad

THIS IS ONE OF OUR FAVORITE GREEN SALADS. ADD COOKED CHICKEN AND IT'S A MAIN DISH.

MAKES: 6 servings

- 1 small head napa cabbage, shredded
- ¼ head iceberg lettuce, shredded
- ½ pound fresh bean sprouts
- 1 cup thinly sliced fresh mushrooms
- 1 cup toasted slivered almonds
- 1 cup crispy Chinese noodles
- 1 recipe Asian Salad Dressing

ONE In a large salad bowl combine napa cabbage, iceberg lettuce, bean sprouts, mushrooms, almonds, and Chinese noodles. Drizzle Asian Salad Dressing over salad; toss to coat.

ASIAN SALAD DRESSING: In a bowl combine ¼ cup soy sauce, ¼ cup white wine or rice vinegar, ¼ cup sugar, 1 tablespoon peanut butter, 1 tablespoon grated fresh ginger, and ½ teaspoon dried coriander, crushed; whisk until smooth. Slowly drizzle in ½ cup vegetable oil, whisking until thickened.

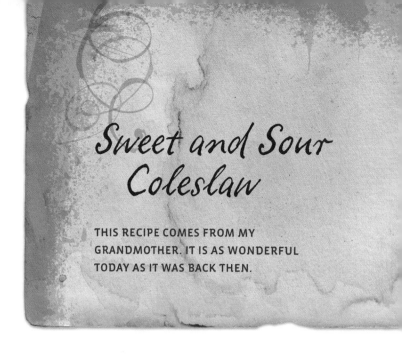

Sweet and Sour Coleslaw

THIS RECIPE COMES FROM MY GRANDMOTHER. IT IS AS WONDERFUL TODAY AS IT WAS BACK THEN.

MAKES: 4 servings

- 3 tablespoons olive oil
- 2 tablespoons apricot or peach preserves
- 2 tablespoons cider vinegar
- 1 tablespoon ketchup
- 1 teaspoon dry mustard
- ½ teaspoon salt
- 4 cups packaged shredded cabbage with carrot (coleslaw mix)
- 2 green onions, thinly sliced

ONE In a large bowl whisk together oil, preserves, vinegar, ketchup, mustard, and salt. Add coleslaw mix and green onion; toss to coat. Serve immediately or cover and refrigerate.

Steamed Broccoli Salad with Pine Nuts and Raisins

PINE NUTS AND RAISINS ADD A SWEET-SALTY TWIST TO BROCCOLI.

MAKES: 4 to 6 servings

1½ pounds broccoli florets

¼ cup pine nuts

¼ cup raisins

2 tablespoons extra-virgin olive oil

1½ tablespoons cider vinegar

1 teaspoon minced fresh garlic

1 teaspoon salt

½ teaspoon black pepper

¼ teaspoon red pepper flakes (optional)

ONE In a saucepan cook broccoli, covered, in 1 inch of water for 5 to 8 minutes or until broccoli is tender and bright green; drain.

TWO Meanwhile, to toast pine nuts, place them in a large skillet. Cook and stir over medium-high heat for 2 to 3 minutes or until golden; cool.

THREE In a large salad bowl combine steamed broccoli, toasted pine nuts, raisins, oil, vinegar, garlic, salt, black pepper, and, if desired, red pepper flakes. Toss to combine. Serve immediately or cover and refrigerate.

Cucumber-Onion Salad

CUCUMBERS AND ONIONS TURN MILD WHEN SOAKED IN SALT. SOUR CREAM PERFECTLY BALANCES THE VINEGAR AND DILL.

MAKES: 4 servings

- 1 large cucumber, peeled and thinly sliced
- 1 medium onion, thinly sliced
- 2 teaspoons salt
- ½ cup sour cream
- 1 tablespoon cider vinegar
- 1 tablespoon dried dill
- ½ teaspoon black pepper
- 2 drops bottled hot pepper sauce

ONE Place cucumber and onion slices in a large bowl; sprinkle with salt. Let stand 30 minutes. Drain off liquid.

TWO In a small bowl combine sour cream, vinegar, dill, black pepper, and hot pepper sauce. Stir into cucumber and onion mixture. Cover and refrigerate at least 1 hour before serving.

Tomato-Artichoke Heart Salad with Blue Cheese Dressing

I'VE HAD HUSBANDS CALL AND THANK ME FOR TEACHING THEIR WIVES HOW TO MAKE THIS SALAD! IT'S A WINNER.

MAKES: 6 servings

- 6 medium ripe tomatoes
- 2 teaspoons salt
- 1 teaspoon black pepper
- ½ cup freshly squeezed lemon juice
- 6 canned artichoke hearts, drained
- 6 lettuce leaves (such as leafy green, red-tipped, or butterhead)
- 1 recipe Blue Cheese Dressing
- 6 sprigs fresh parsley

ONE To make tomato cups, cut ¼ inch off the top of each tomato. Use a spoon to scoop out the pulp; set pulp aside. Sprinkle insides of each tomato cup with salt and pepper.

TWO Drizzle lemon juice generously over and inside each artichoke heart. (This will eliminate any canned flavor.) Place one artichoke heart inside each tomato cup. Chop the reserved tomato pulp; fill in tomato cups around the artichoke hearts.

THREE Place one lettuce leaf on each of 6 salad plates. Top each with a tomato cup. Spoon Blue Cheese Dressing generously over tomato cups. Garnish each serving with parsley.

PLAN AHEAD: Prepare through Step Two. Cover and refrigerate tomato cups until time to serve. Continue according to Step Three.

BLUE CHEESE DRESSING: Stir together 1½ cups mayonnaise, 1½ cups sour cream, and 1 cup crumbled blue cheese until smooth. Stir in 1 cup buttermilk, 2 teaspoons Worcestershire sauce, and 2 teaspoons minced fresh garlic. Cover and refrigerate up to 2 weeks.

Greek Potato Salad

FETA CHEESE MAKES THE PERFECT PARTNER FOR POTATOES. ADDING FRESH LEMON JUICE TO THE WARM POTATOES HELPS THEM SOAK UP THE MAXIMUM AMOUNT OF FLAVOR.

MAKES: 4 servings

- 2 pounds new potatoes
- ½ cup freshly squeezed lemon juice
- 1 cup sliced, pitted black olives
- 10 green onions, thinly sliced
- ½ cup diced pimiento
- 1 tablespoon dried oregano, crushed
- ½ cup olive oil
- ½ cup vegetable oil
- 2 teaspoons salt (or to taste)
- ½ teaspoon black pepper
- 4 ounces feta cheese, crumbled

ONE Wash potatoes but do not peel. In a large saucepan boil potatoes in enough water to cover until tender. When cool enough to handle, cut potatoes into bite-size chunks; place in a large bowl. Sprinkle warm potatoes with ¼ cup of the lemon juice. Stir in olives, green onion, pimiento, and oregano.

TWO For dressing, in a small bowl whisk together the remaining ¼ cup lemon juice, olive oil, vegetable oil, salt, and pepper. Drizzle dressing over potato mixture; toss to coat. Cover and refrigerate. Just before serving, fold in feta cheese.

Pineapple-Coconut-Carrot Salad with Coriander Dressing

SOMETIMES I ENHANCE THIS SALAD WITH RAISINS OR CHOPPED APPLES.

MAKES: 6 to 8 servings

½ pound carrots, grated

1 15-ounce can pineapple tidbits, drained

1 cup shredded coconut

2 tablespoons powdered sugar

1 recipe Coriander Dressing

ONE In a large salad bowl combine carrot, pineapple, coconut, and powdered sugar. Pour Coriander Dressing over carrot mixture; toss to coat. Serve immediately or cover and refrigerate up to 2 hours.

CORIANDER DRESSING: In a small bowl whisk together ½ cup mayonnaise; ½ cup sour cream; 2 tablespoons milk; 2 teaspoons dried coriander, crushed; and 1 teaspoon sugar.

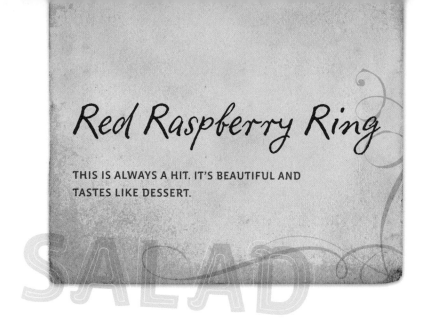

Red Raspberry Ring

THIS IS ALWAYS A HIT. IT'S BEAUTIFUL AND TASTES LIKE DESSERT.

MAKES: 6 to 8 servings

- 1 10 ounce package frozen raspberries, thawed
- 2 3-ounce packages red raspberry gelatin
- 2 cups boiling water
- 1 pint vanilla ice cream
- 1 6-ounce can frozen pink lemonade concentrate, thawed
- ¼ cup chopped pecans
- 1 cup sweetened whipped cream

ONE Drain raspberries, reserving the juice; set aside. In a large bowl dissolve gelatin in boiling water. Add ice cream by spoonfuls, stirring until melted. Stir in lemonade concentrate and reserved raspberry juice. Cover and chill until partially set. Stir in raspberries and pecans.

TWO Pour gelatin mixture into a 2-quart ring mold. Cover and refrigerate until firm.

THREE To unmold easily, press a warm, wet dishcloth around mold to slightly loosen gelatin. Unmold salad onto a serving platter. Garnish with whipped cream.

Five-Cup Fruit Salad

IT'S SO EASY TO KEEP THIS INGREDIENT LIST IN YOUR HEAD—
YOU CAN GRAB THE ITEMS QUICKLY IN THE GROCERY STORE.

MAKES: 4 to 6 servings

1   cup shredded coconut

1   cup miniature marshmallows

1   8-ounce can pineapple
    tidbits, drained

1   8-ounce can mandarin
    oranges, drained

1   cup sour cream

ONE In a large salad bowl combine coconut, marshmallows, pineapple, and mandarin oranges. Gently stir in sour cream.

TWO Cover and refrigerate for several hours before serving.

Lucky Lime-and-Pineapple Congealed Salad

CARBONATION ADDS SPARKLE TO THIS MOLDED SALAD. CREAM CHEESE SMOOTHS THE TANGY LIME AND PINEAPPLE FLAVORS.

SALAD

MAKES: 12 to 15 servings

- 2 cups miniature marshmallows
- 8 ounces lemon-lime carbonated beverage
- 1 8-ounce package cream cheese, softened
- 1 3-ounce package lime gelatin
- 1 20-ounce can crushed pineapple, undrained
- 1 cup frozen whipped dessert topping, thawed
- ¾ cup chopped pecans

ONE In a saucepan combine marshmallows and carbonated beverage. Cook and stir over medium heat until marshmallows melt. Add cream cheese and gelatin, stirring until gelatin dissolves. Remove saucepan from heat; stir in undrained pineapple, whipped dessert topping, and pecans.

TWO Pour gelatin mixture into a 13×9×2-inch baking dish. Cover and refrigerate until firm.

Orange Salad Delight

CHEDDAR CHEESE BRINGS RICHNESS AND DEPTH TO THIS
ORANGE-PINEAPPLE SALAD.

MAKES: 6 to 8 servings

- 1 16-ounce can crushed pineapple, undrained
- 1 3-ounce package orange gelatin
- ¼ cup sugar
- 1 cup shredded cheddar cheese
- 1 cup chopped pecans
- 1 cup heavy cream, whipped, or 2 cups frozen whipped topping, thawed

ONE Drain pineapple, reserving the juice. Add enough water to juice to equal 1 cup.

TWO In a saucepan combine pineapple juice mixture, orange gelatin, and sugar. Cook and stir over medium heat until gelatin dissolves. Remove saucepan from heat. Stir in pineapple, cheese, and pecans. Fold in whipped cream.

THREE Pour into a 2-quart mold. Cover and refrigerate about 4 hours or until firm.

Simple Tortellini Salad

MY GRANDSON, STEVEN, LOVES THIS SALAD AND MAKES IT FOR HIS FAMILY TOO.

MAKES: 6 servings

- 1 pound fresh or frozen tri-color cheese-filled tortellini
- 2 cups grape or small cherry tomatoes
- ¾ to 1 cup bottled Italian salad dressing*

ONE Cook tortellini according to package directions; drain. Rinse with cool water; drain well.

TWO Place cooked tortellini in a large salad bowl; add tomatoes. Pour salad dressing over tortellini and tomatoes; toss to coat. Serve immediately or cover and refrigerate.

*NOTE: As salad sits in the refrigerator, it will absorb the salad dressing. If salad looks dry when you're ready to serve, add additional salad dressing.

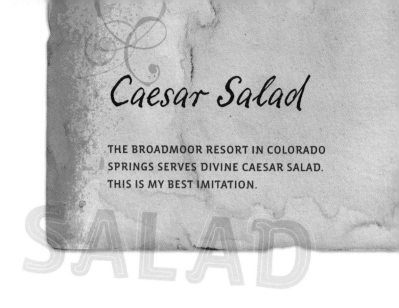

Caesar Salad

THE BROADMOOR RESORT IN COLORADO
SPRINGS SERVES DIVINE CAESAR SALAD.
THIS IS MY BEST IMITATION.

MAKES: 6 servings

- ¼ cup egg substitute
- 3 tablespoons red wine vinegar
- 2 tablespoons freshly squeezed lemon juice
- 1 tablespoon Dijon mustard
- 1 tablespoon anchovy paste (optional)
- 1 teaspoon minced fresh garlic
- 1 teaspoon salt
- ½ teaspoon black pepper
- ¾ cup olive oil
- ¼ cup vegetable oil
- 1 head romaine or leafy green lettuce, torn into bite-size pieces
- 3 cups Croutons (page 166)
- 1 cup grated Parmesan cheese

ONE In a large salad bowl whisk together egg substitute, vinegar, lemon juice, mustard, anchovy paste (if desired), garlic, salt, and pepper. In a small bowl combine olive oil and vegetable oil; drizzle into egg mixture in a slow, steady stream, whisking constantly until combined.

TWO Add torn romaine to salad bowl; toss to coat. Add Croutons and Parmesan cheese; toss to combine.

Endive and Apple Salad

GREEN APPLES, RED CRANBERRIES, AND OTHER COLORFUL
INGREDIENTS MAKE THIS A FESTIVE SALAD FOR THE HOLIDAYS.

MAKES: 4 servings

- ½ cup freshly squeezed lemon juice
- ¼ cup olive oil
- 2 tablespoons balsamic vinegar
- 1 teaspoon salt
- ½ teaspoon black pepper
- 5 heads Belgian endive, ends trimmed and cut crosswise into 1-inch slices
- ¼ pound Gruyère cheese, cut into ½-inch pieces
- 1 green apple, sliced
- 1 large avocado, peeled, seeded, and sliced
- ¼ cup dried cranberries

ONE For vinaigrette, in a small bowl whisk together lemon juice, oil, vinegar, salt, and pepper. Set aside.

TWO In a large bowl combine endive, cheese, apple, avocado, and cranberries. Drizzle vinaigrette over salad; toss to coat. Arrange on a large serving platter.

PLAN AHEAD: Prepare vinaigrette up to 1 week ahead. Cover and refrigerate. Shake well before using.

Spinach Salad

WITH BAGGED, TRIPLE-WASHED BABY SPINACH, THIS SALAD IS A SNAP. IT'S A GOOD WAY TO GET FRESH SPINACH DOWN YOUR KIDS.

MAKES: 4 to 6 servings

6   to 8 pieces bacon, slivered

2   1-pound bags prewashed spinach

8   ounces fresh mushrooms, sliced

1   cup grated Parmesan cheese

3   or 4 green onions, thinly sliced

1   recipe Balsamic Maple Vinaigrette (page 199)

ONE In a large skillet cook bacon until crisp. Drain on paper towels.

TWO Tear spinach into bite-size pieces; place in a large salad bowl. Add mushrooms, Parmesan cheese, bacon, and green onion; toss to combine. Drizzle with desired amount of Balsamic Maple Vinaigrette; toss to coat.

Apple-Walnut-Raisin Spinach Salad

SERVED ON A LARGE PLATTER, THIS SALAD MAKES A BEAUTIFUL CENTERPIECE. ORANGE CURRIED DRESSING ADDS SWEET AND SOUR FLAVORS TO THE SPINACH.

MAKES: 8 servings

- 6 to 8 slices bacon, slivered
- 1 1-pound bag prewashed spinach
- 2 apples, chopped or sliced
- 1 cup golden raisins
- ½ cup coarsely chopped walnuts or pecans
- 3 green onions, thinly sliced
- 1 recipe Orange Curried Dressing

ONE In a large skillet cook bacon until crisp. Drain on paper towels.

TWO Arrange the spinach on a large serving platter. Top with apple, raisins, nuts, bacon, and green onion. Drizzle with desired amount of Orange Curried Dressing.

ORANGE CURRIED DRESSING: In a blender or food processor combine ½ cup cider vinegar, ¼ cup sugar, 1 teaspoon curry powder, 1 teaspoon dry mustard, 1 teaspoon salt, and ¼ teaspoon black pepper. With machine running, slowly pour in 1 cup vegetable oil. Add 1 tablespoon orange marmalade (or to taste); pulse a few times to combine but not enough to lose the texture of the marmalade. Cover and refrigerate up to 1 month.

Mixed Field Greens with Candied Pecans and Goat Cheese

THIS IS OUR COOKING SCHOOL'S SIGNATURE SALAD. WE FEEL LIKE WE HAVE TAUGHT HALF OF TEXAS TO MAKE IT!

MAKES: 6 servings

- 6 to 8 slices bacon, slivered
- 8 to 10 cups baby field greens or torn leaf lettuce
- 1 cup crumbled chèvre (goat cheese) or 4 ounces, sliced
- 1 recipe Balsamic Maple Vinaigrette
- 1 recipe Candied Pecans

ONE In a large skillet cook bacon until crisp. Drain on paper towels.

TWO In a large salad bowl toss together field greens, bacon, and goat cheese. Drizzle with desired amount of Balsamic Maple Vinaigrette; toss to coat. Add Candied Pecans; toss to combine.

BALSAMIC MAPLE VINAIGRETTE: In a large jar with a tight-fitting lid combine 1 cup vegetable oil; ½ cup balsamic vinegar; ½ cup olive oil; ¼ cup pure maple syrup; 2 tablespoons Dijon mustard; 1 large shallot, minced; ½ teaspoon salt; and ¼ teaspoon black pepper. Cover and shake well. Refrigerate up to 1 month. Shake well before using. Makes about 2¼ cups.

CANDIED PECANS: Place ½ cup packed brown sugar and ¼ cup water in a heavy skillet. Cook over medium-low heat, stirring constantly, until sugar dissolves. Add 2 cups pecan halves. Cook, stirring constantly, about 5 minutes or until all water evaporates. (Be careful not to burn pecans.) Spread pecans in a single layer on a baking sheet. Let stand until cool and dry. Store in an airtight container up to 2 weeks.

Blue Cheese Wedge Salad

WE LOVE TO ORDER THIS SALAD AT OUR FAVORITE STEAK HOUSE.
HOMEMADE BLUE CHEESE DRESSING MAKES THIS VERSION SPECIAL.

MAKES: 8 servings

- 2 **small to medium heads iceberg lettuce**
- 1 **to 1½ cups Blue Cheese Dressing (page 183)**
- 2 **teaspoons black pepper**

ONE Cut each head of lettuce into 4 wedges. Place 1 wedge on each of 8 salad plates.

TWO Spoon Blue Cheese Dressing over lettuce wedges; sprinkle with pepper.

vegetables & fruit

Incredible Baked Beans

THESE ARE A STAPLE AT OUR HOUSE FOR COOKOUTS.

MAKES: 8 to 10 servings

Nonstick cooking spray

½ pound bacon, slivered

1 cup chopped onion

1 cup chopped bell pepper

2 28-ounce cans baked beans

1 cup packed brown sugar

1 cup ketchup

¼ cup Worcestershire sauce

ONE Preheat oven to 350°F. Coat a 13×9×2-inch baking dish with cooking spray.

TWO In a large saucepan cook bacon over medium-high heat until crisp. Remove bacon with a slotted spoon; set aside.

THREE Add onion and bell pepper to drippings in saucepan. Cook and stir until tender; drain off fat. Stir in beans, brown sugar, ketchup, Worcestershire sauce, and cooked bacon. Transfer to prepared baking dish.

FOUR Bake, uncovered, for 2 hours. Beans will be soupy when they come out of the oven but will thicken in a few minutes.

Creamed Corn Casserole

NIBLET CORN, DICED GREEN CHILES, AND MELTED CHEESE COMBINE IN A CREAMY CUSTARD. HEARTY ENOUGH TO SERVE WITH STEAKS.

MAKES: 6 servings

Nonstick cooking spray

1 15-ounce can creamed corn

1 12-ounce package corn bread mix

1 cup frozen corn

1 cup milk

½ cup shredded cheddar cheese

2 eggs, beaten

1 4-ounce can diced green chile peppers, undrained

¼ cup vegetable oil

¼ cup finely chopped onion

1 teaspoon sugar

1 teaspoon salt

½ teaspoon black pepper

ONE Preheat oven to 375°F. Coat a 1½-quart baking dish with cooking spray.

TWO In a bowl combine creamed corn, corn bread mix, frozen corn, milk, cheese, eggs, undrained chile peppers, oil, onion, sugar, salt, and black pepper. Beat with a wooden spoon until smooth. Pour corn mixture into prepared baking dish.

THREE Bake, uncovered, for 20 to 25 minutes or until center is almost set.

Stir-Fried Bok Choy

FIND BOK CHOY IN ASIAN MARKETS OR SPECIAL
GROCERY STORES.

MAKES: 4 to 6 servings

3 tablespoons olive oil

1 tablespoon toasted sesame oil

1 head bok choy (about
1 pound), trimmed, washed,
and cut into quarters

3 cloves garlic, sliced

5 green onions, sliced
lengthwise into thin strips

2 tablespoons oyster sauce

2 tablespoons freshly squeezed
lime juice

1 tablespoon soy sauce

2 dashes sugar

Salt

Black pepper

ONE Preheat olive oil and sesame oil in a wok or
large skillet over high heat. Add bok choy and garlic;
stir-fry until crisp-tender. Add green onion, oyster
sauce, lime juice, soy sauce, and sugar; toss to coat.
Season to taste with salt and pepper.

Potatoes Cordon Bleu

THIS DISH IS AN OFTEN-REQUESTED RECIPE AT OUR CULINARY SCHOOL.

MAKES: 8 servings

- 2 cups heavy cream
- 2 cups half-and-half or light cream
- 3 teaspoons chopped fresh garlic
- 3 teaspoons salt
- ½ teaspoon black pepper
- 1 bay leaf
- 3 to 3½ pounds russet potatoes, peeled and cut into ⅛-inch slices
- 1½ cups sour cream
- 1 cup shredded Parmesan cheese

ONE Preheat oven to 350°F. In a large saucepan combine heavy cream, half-and-half, garlic, salt, pepper, and bay leaf. Bring to simmering over medium-low heat. Add potato slices to saucepan. Simmer, uncovered, for 10 minutes. Remove bay leaf.

TWO Spread ¾ cup of the sour cream into the bottom of a 13×9×2-inch baking dish. Cover with potato slices and cream mixture. Top potatoes with the remaining ¾ cup sour cream; sprinkle with Parmesan cheese.

THREE Bake, uncovered, about 20 minutes or until hot and bubbly and lightly browned.

PLAN AHEAD: Prepare through Step Two up to 1 day ahead. Cover and refrigerate. Preheat oven. Uncover and continue according to Step Three.

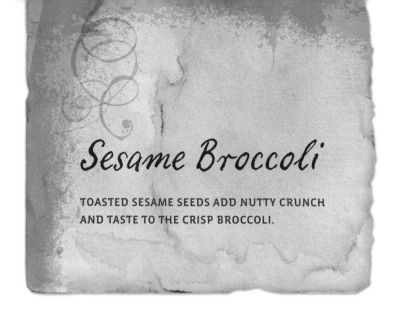

Sesame Broccoli

TOASTED SESAME SEEDS ADD NUTTY CRUNCH AND TASTE TO THE CRISP BROCCOLI.

MAKES: 4 servings

- 1 tablespoon vegetable oil
- 1 tablespoon toasted sesame oil
- 1 to 1¼ pounds fresh broccoli florets
- 2 tablespoons minced fresh ginger
- 2 teaspoons minced fresh garlic
- 1 teaspoon salt
- 2 tablespoons water
- 1 tablespoon sesame seeds, toasted

ONE Preheat vegetable oil and sesame oil in a wok or large skillet. Add broccoli florets; stir-fry for 2 minutes. Add ginger, garlic, and salt; stir-fry 2 minutes more. Add water; cover and steam for 2 minutes.

TWO Place broccoli on a serving platter; sprinkle with sesame seeds.

Roasted Vegetables

SO BRIGHT AND PRETTY, THIS COULD EASILY BE A CENTERPIECE AT DINNER.

MAKES: 4 to 6 servings

1 zucchini, cut into bite-size pieces

1 yellow summer squash, cut into bite-size pieces

1 red bell pepper, cut into strips

1 yellow bell pepper, cut into strips

8 ounces fresh mushrooms, sliced

1 medium onion, sliced and separated into rings

3 tablespoons olive oil

1 teaspoon dried thyme, crushed

1 teaspoon salt

½ teaspoon black pepper

ONE Preheat oven to 450°F. Place zucchini, summer squash, bell peppers, mushrooms, and onion rings in a large bowl. Add oil, thyme, salt, and black pepper; toss to coat. Arrange vegetables in a single layer on a large baking sheet.

TWO Roast vegetables, uncovered, about 30 minutes or until lightly browned and tender, stirring once or twice.

Fresh Chunky Tomato Salsa

USING CANNED TOMATOES GUARANTEES CONSISTENCY EVERY TIME. SERVE WITH CORN CHIPS OR OVER GRILLED CHICKEN OR GRILLED VEGETABLES.

MAKES: 4½ cups

- 1 28-ounce can diced tomatoes, undrained
- 1 7-ounce can diced green chile peppers, undrained
- ¼ cup chopped fresh cilantro
- 3 green onions, finely chopped
- 1 fresh jalapeño chile pepper, seeded and chopped (optional)
- 1 tablespoon balsamic vinegar or freshly squeezed lemon juice
- 1 tablespoon vegetable oil
- 1 teaspoon salt (or to taste)

ONE Place undrained tomatoes in a food processor. Cover and process until desired consistency. Transfer to a large bowl. Stir in undrained chile peppers, cilantro, green onions, jalapeño pepper (if desired), vinegar, oil, and salt.

Lemon-Butter Edamame

EDAMAME IS ANOTHER WORD FOR SOYBEANS. THEY ARE FIRM AND BRIGHT GREEN, AND KIDS LOVE TO EAT THEM.

MAKES: 6 servings

1 **16-ounce package frozen shelled edamame (soybeans)**

1 **cup water**

1 **teaspoon salt**

2 **tablespoons freshly squeezed lemon juice**

1 **tablespoon lemon zest**

1 **tablespoon butter**

ONE In a saucepan bring edamame, water, and salt to simmering. Cover and simmer for 5 minutes.

TWO Drain edamame; return to saucepan. Stir in lemon juice, lemon zest, and butter.

Apricot-Glazed Carrots

EVEN KIDS WILL LOVE THESE SWEET CARROTS.

MAKES: 4 to 6 servings

- 1 16-ounce package peeled fresh baby carrots
- 1 tablespoon salt
  Water
- ¼ cup apricot preserves
- 2 tablespoons butter
- 1½ teaspoons grated fresh ginger
  Chopped fresh parsley, (optional)

ONE Place carrots and salt in a saucepan. Add just enough water to barely cover the carrots. Bring to boiling over high heat. Turn heat to medium. Cover and simmer for 5 to 8 minutes or until tender.

TWO Drain carrots; return to saucepan. Stir in preserves, butter, and ginger; heat through. If desired, sprinkle with chopped fresh parsley.

Italian Green Beans and Potatoes

ITALIAN GREEN BEANS SEEM TO HAVE MORE OF A DISTINCT GARDEN-GROWN FLAVOR THAN REGULAR CANNED GREEN BEANS.

VEGETABLES

MAKES: 6 servings

- 3 new potatoes
- 2 15-ounce cans cut green Italian beans, undrained
- 1 15-ounce can diced tomatoes, undrained
- ⅓ cup chopped onion
- 2 teaspoons salt
- 1 teaspoon dried Italian mixed herbs, crushed
- ½ teaspoon black pepper
- ¾ cup grated Parmesan cheese

ONE Cut each potato into 8 pieces. Place in a 4- to 6-quart Dutch oven or large saucepan along with undrained green beans, undrained tomatoes, onion, salt, Italian herbs, and pepper. Cover and simmer for about 25 minutes or until potatoes are very tender.

TWO Transfer vegetables to a serving bowl; sprinkle with Parmesan cheese.

Spinach with Lemon and Parmesan

TANGY LEMON AND PUNGENT PARMESAN CHEESE COMPLEMENT THE MELLOW FLAVOR OF SPINACH.

MAKES: 4 to 6 servings

- 2 tablespoons olive oil
- 2 large shallots, thinly sliced
- 3 1-pound bags prewashed spinach
- 2 teaspoons freshly squeezed lemon juice
- ½ cup shredded Parmesan cheese
- ½ teaspoon salt
- ½ teaspoon black pepper

ONE Preheat oil in a large soup pot. Add shallot; cook and stir for 3 to 4 minutes or until golden. Add spinach and lemon juice, tossing with tongs to combine.

TWO Cook about 5 minutes, stirring occasionally, until spinach is tender but still bright green. Stir in Parmesan cheese, salt, and pepper.

Warm Cherry Tomato Salad

SERVE THIS WONDERFUL SALAD HOT, WARM, OR COLD.

MAKES: 4 to 6 servings

- 2 tablespoons olive oil
- 2 teaspoons minced fresh garlic
- 2 pints cherry tomatoes
- 6 green onions, bias-sliced, or ½ cup finely chopped onion
- 2 tablespoons red wine vinegar
- 1 teaspoon salt
- ½ teaspoon black pepper
- ½ cup chopped fresh parsley

ONE Preheat oil in a large skillet over medium-high heat. Add garlic; cook and stir for 2 minutes.

TWO Add tomatoes and green onion; cook and stir until tomato skins begin to burst. Stir in vinegar, salt, and pepper. Remove skillet from heat. Add parsley; toss to combine.

Sweet Potatoes and Apples

SWEET POTATOES AND APPLES PAIR
PERFECTLY, AND APPLE JUICE ADDS
EVEN MORE SWEETNESS AND FLAVOR.

MAKES: 8 servings

- 4 large sweet potatoes
- Nonstick cooking spray
- 3 large cooking apples
- ½ cup packed brown sugar
- ⅓ cup granulated sugar
- 1 teaspoon ground cinnamon
- ½ cup butter
- 1 6-ounce can frozen apple juice concentrate, thawed

ONE Preheat oven to 375°F. Bake sweet potatoes for about 45 minutes or until tender. Let potatoes cool on a wire rack. Coat a 2-quart baking dish with cooking spray.

TWO Peel the baked sweet potatoes and apples; cut into ¼-inch slices. Combine brown sugar, granulated sugar, and cinnamon. Layer potatoes and apples in the prepared baking dish, sprinkling each layer with some of the sugar-cinnamon mixture and dotting with butter. Pour apple juice concentrate over all.

THREE Bake, uncovered, for about 45 minutes or until apples are very tender.

PLAN AHEAD: Prepare up to 2 days ahead. Cover and refrigerate. Preheat oven. Uncover and reheat for 30 minutes.

Garlic-Roasted Potatoes

THIS IS THE CURRENT FAVORITE POTATO RECIPE AT OUR HOUSE. IT'S EASY AND FULL OF FLAVOR—ALWAYS THE PERFECT COMBINATION.

VEGETABLES

MAKES: 6 servings

- 3 pounds new potatoes, unpeeled
- ¼ cup olive oil
- 2 tablespoons minced fresh garlic
- 2 teaspoons salt (or to taste)
- ½ teaspoon black pepper (or to taste)

ONE Preheat oven to 400°F. Place potatoes on a large baking sheet; drizzle with oil. Sprinkle with garlic, salt, and pepper; toss to coat.

TWO Bake, uncovered, for 25 to 30 minutes or until golden brown, stirring halfway through roasting.

Asparagus Baked with Cheese

KIDS SEEM TO LIKE VEGETABLES IF THEY HAVE CHEESE MELTED ON TOP. THIS RECIPE IS A GOOD WAY TO INTRODUCE CHILDREN TO ASPARAGUS.

MAKES: 6 servings

- 2 **pounds fresh asparagus spears**
- ½ **cup butter, melted**
- 1 **envelope dry onion soup mix**
- 1 **cup shredded mozzarella cheese**

ONE Preheat oven to 350°F. Arrange asparagus spears in an 8-inch square baking dish. Combine melted butter and onion soup mix; drizzle over asparagus. Sprinkle with cheese.

TWO Bake, uncovered, for about 10 minutes or until asparagus is tender and cheese is hot and bubbly.

Fresh Cranberry-Orange Compote

MAKE THIS BEAUTIFUL JEWEL-TONE SAUCE FOR
THANKSGIVING AND ALL YEAR-ROUND.

FRUIT

MAKES: 8 servings

- 1   12-ounce package fresh cranberries
- 1   cup sugar
- ¾   cup water

    Zest and juice of 1 orange

ONE In a saucepan combine cranberries, sugar, and water. Simmer over medium-high heat for 20 minutes. While simmering, use a wooden spoon to crush the cranberries against the sides of the saucepan, releasing their juices. Stir in orange zest and orange juice. Cool. Cover and refrigerate.

PLAN AHEAD: Buy extra bags of fresh cranberries during November and December. Place the bags in freezer bags and refrigerate up to 2 months or freeze up to 1 year.

Mango Salsa

JARRED MANGOES ARE THE WAY TO GO SINCE SLICING FRESH ONES IS TIME-CONSUMING. BUT IF YOU HAPPEN TO HAVE FRESH MANGOES, THIS IS A GOOD WAY TO USE THEM. SERVE SALSA OVER GRILLED CHICKEN, PORK, OR FISH.

MAKES: about 4 cups

- 1½ cups chopped jarred mango slices
- 1 cup diced fresh pineapple
- 1 avocado, diced
- ½ cup diced red onion
- ½ cup chopped fresh cilantro
- ¼ cup freshly squeezed lime juice
- 1 fresh jalapeño chile pepper, seeded and diced
- 2 teaspoons minced fresh garlic
- 1 teaspoon salt (or to taste)
- ½ teaspoon black pepper (or to taste)
- ½ teaspoon chili powder
- ¼ teaspoon ground cumin

ONE In a bowl stir together mango, pineapple, avocado, onion, cilantro, lime juice, jalapeño pepper, garlic, salt, black pepper, chili powder, and cumin.

TWO Cover and refrigerate at least 1 hour to allow flavors to mingle.

FREEZE AHEAD: Freeze salsa in a freezer bag up to 2 months. Defrost completely in refrigerator.

Curried Fruit

THIS ELEGANT FRUIT DISH IS ESPECIALLY DELICIOUS WITH OMELETS, AND IT COMPLEMENTS ALMOST ANY MEAT DISH.

MAKES: 8 servings

- 1   15-ounce can sliced peaches, drained
- 1   15-ounce can apricot halves, drained
- 1   15-ounce can mixed fruit, drained
- 1   15-ounce can pineapple chunks, drained
- 1   cup packed brown sugar
- ½   cup maraschino cherry halves, drained
- 2   teaspoons curry powder
- 1   teaspoon ground cinnamon

ONE In a saucepan stir together peaches, apricot halves, mixed fruit, pineapple chunks, brown sugar, cherries, curry powder, and cinnamon. Simmer 10 minutes, stirring often so mixture doesn't stick and burn. Serve warm.

desserts

Miracle Pecan-Caramel Bars

THE MIRACLE IS HOW EASY THESE ARE TO MAKE.
THE TASTE IS DIVINE.

MAKES: 24 bars

- ½ cup butter, melted
- 1 package yellow cake mix
- 2 8-ounce packages cream cheese, softened
- 1 cup packed brown sugar
- ½ cup chopped pecans

ONE Preheat oven to 350°F.

TWO For crust, in a bowl use a fork to stir together melted butter and dry cake mix. Press crust mixture into the bottom of a 13×9×2-inch baking dish.

THREE Use a mixer to beat together cream cheese and brown sugar; stir in pecans. Spread cream cheese mixture over crust.

FOUR Bake about 20 minutes or until golden brown.

FREEZE AHEAD: Bake bars; cool completely. Cut into bars. Place in a freezer container and freeze up to 2 months.

No-Bake Chocolate Cookies

A BYRD FAMILY HEIRLOOM FOR FOUR GENERATIONS, THESE ARE HALF CANDY, HALF COOKIE, AND THEY PACK WELL FOR TRIPS OR CAMPOUTS. SOMETIMES WE CAN'T HELP EATING THE MIX RIGHT OUT OF THE PAN.

MAKES: 2 dozen cookies

- 2 cups sugar
- ½ cup butter
- ½ cup milk
- ⅓ cup cocoa powder
- 3 cups quick-cooking oats
- ½ cup creamy peanut butter
- 1 teaspoon vanilla

ONE Line 2 large cookie sheets with waxed paper or parchment paper

TWO In a saucepan combine sugar, butter, milk, and cocoa powder. Bring to boiling over medium heat, stirring constantly. Boil for 2 minutes.

THREE Remove saucepan from heat. Stir in oats, peanut butter, and vanilla. Drop by spoonfuls onto prepared cookie sheets. Let stand until firm.

FREEZE AHEAD: Prepare cookies through Step Three. Place in a freezer container and freeze up to 2 months.

Hello Dolly Bars

IT'S EASY TO KEEP THESE INGREDIENTS IN THE PANTRY.

DESSERTS

MAKES: 24 bars

Nonstick cooking spray

2½ cups graham cracker crumbs

½ cup butter, melted

2 cups shredded coconut

2 cups chocolate chips

1 cup chopped pecans

1 15-ounce can sweetened condensed milk

ONE Preheat oven to 350°F. Coat a 13×9×2-inch baking pan with cooking spray.

TWO Place graham cracker crumbs in the bottom of the prepared pan; drizzle with butter. Mix with a fork and spread evenly in the botom of the pan. Layer with coconut, chocolate chips, and pecans. Drizzle sweetened condensed milk over the top.

THREE Bake about 25 minutes or until golden brown.

FREEZE AHEAD: Bake bars; cool completely. Cut into bars. Place in a freezer container and freeze up to 2 months.

Frozen Yogurt Pops

KEEP THESE ON HAND FOR AN INSTANT DESSERT.

MAKES: 6 pops

2   cups plain yogurt

1   6-ounce can frozen orange juice concentrate, thawed

1   teaspoon vanilla

6   4-ounce paper cups

6   wooden popsicle sticks

ONE Combine yogurt, orange juice concentrate, and vanilla; divide among paper cups. Insert a popsicle stick into the center of each cup. Place cups on a tray or baking sheet. Freeze until solid.

TWO To serve, peel away the paper cup.

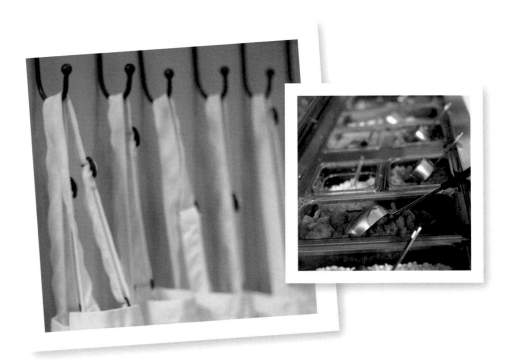

Instant Sopaipillas

PASTRY CHEFS HAVE TOLD ME THESE ARE THE BEST SOPAIPILLAS EVER!

MAKES: 16 sopaipillas

½ cup sugar

1 teaspoon ground cinnamon

1 loaf frozen bread dough, thawed

2 cups vegetable oil

ONE In a small bowl combine sugar and cinnamon; set aside.

TWO Cut bread dough into 16 even pieces. In a deep, heavy skillet heat ½ inch vegetable oil over medium heat. Fry dough pieces, a few at a time, in hot oil until golden brown, turning once. Drain on paper towels.

THREE Roll fried dough pieces in the cinnamon-sugar mixture. Serve warm.

Easy Apple Crisp

A CRUNCHY, BUTTERY TOPPING OVER APPLES CREATES A FAVORITE TASTE DUO.

MAKES: 6 servings

Nonstick cooking spray

- 1 cup quick-cooking oats
- ⅔ cup packed brown sugar
- ½ cup all-purpose flour
- ½ cup butter, melted
- 1 20-ounce can apple pie filling

Ice cream or whipped cream

ONE Preheat oven to 350°F. Coat an 8×8×2-inch baking dish with cooking spray.

TWO In a bowl use a fork to combine oats, brown sugar, and flour. Stir in melted butter. Press two-thirds of the oat mixture into the prepared cake pan.

THREE Spoon pie filling over oat mixture. Sprinkle with the remaining oat mixture.

FOUR Bake for 30 to 35 minutes or until lightly browned. Serve warm with ice cream or whipped cream.

FREEZE AHEAD: Prepare through Step Three. Cover with plastic wrap and foil. Freeze up to 2 months. Defrost completely. Preheat oven. Remove plastic wrap and foil and continue according to Step Four.

EASY PEACH CRISP: Substitute peach pie filling for the apple pie filling.

Bread Pudding

RAISINS AND COCONUT ADD RICH FLAVOR
TO THIS ALREADY-DECADENT DESSERT.

MAKES: 8 to 10 servings

Nonstick cooking spray

8 cups stale French or sourdough bread cubes

2 cups milk

1½ cups sugar

⅓ cup butter, melted

3 eggs, beaten

½ cup raisins

½ cup shredded coconut

2 teaspoons vanilla

1 teaspoon almond flavoring

1 teaspoon ground cinnamon

1 recipe Butter Sauce

ONE Preheat oven to 350°F. Coat a 13×9×2-inch baking pan with cooking spray.

TWO In a large bowl stir together bread cubes and milk. Stir in sugar, melted butter, eggs, raisins, coconut, vanilla, almond flavoring, and cinnamon. Pour into prepared pan.

THREE Bake about 1 hour or until middle is set and top is golden brown. Serve with Butter Sauce.

FREEZE AHEAD: Prepare through Step Two. Cover with plastic wrap and foil. Freeze up to 2 months. Defrost completely in refrigerator. Preheat oven. Remove plastic wrap and foil and continue according to Step Three.

BUTTER SAUCE: In a small saucepan combine ½ cup butter and ¼ cup light-colored corn syrup. Cook and stir over low heat until butter melts. Add 1 cup sifted powdered sugar, stirring until sugar dissolves. Remove from heat; stir in 1 teaspoon vanilla.

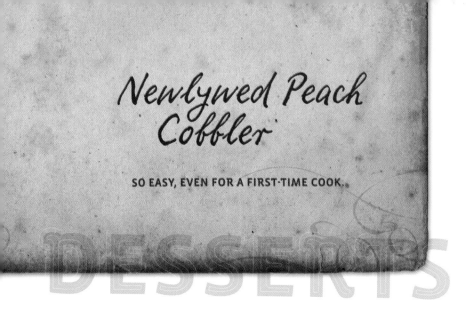

Newlywed Peach Cobbler

SO EASY, EVEN FOR A FIRST-TIME COOK.

DESSERTS

MAKES: 6 servings

Nonstick cooking spray

- 1 28-ounce can sliced peaches
- 1 teaspoon ground cinnamon
- ½ teaspoon ground allspice
- 1 cup all-purpose flour
- 1 cup sugar
- ¼ cup butter, cut up

ONE Preheat oven to 350°F. Coat a 9×9×2-inch baking dish with cooking spray. Drain peaches, reserving juice.

TWO Place drained peaches in the bottom of the prepared baking dish; sprinkle with cinnamon and allspice. In a bowl stir together flour and sugar; pour evenly over peaches. Pour reserved peach juice evenly over the top; dot with butter.

THREE Bake about 35 minutes or until golden brown.

FREEZE AHEAD: Prepare through Step Two. Cover with plastic wrap and foil. Freeze up to 2 months. Defrost completely in refrigerator. Preheat oven. Remove plastic wrap and foil and continue according to Step Three.

Baked Fruit

THIS QUICK RECIPE IS PERFECT WHEN YOU NEED A LAST-MINUTE DESSERT. TOP WITH A SCOOP OF VANILLA ICE CREAM FOR A DECADENT TREAT.

MAKES: 6 servings

2 tablespoons butter

2 tablespoons packed brown sugar

1 teaspoon ground cinnamon

6 fresh peaches, apples, and/or pears

ONE Preheat oven to 375°F. Place butter, brown sugar, and cinnamon in a large flat baking dish. Heat in oven about 5 minutes or until butter melts; stir to combine. Cut fruit in half; remove seed or core. Place fruit, cut sides down, on top of melted butter mixture.

TWO Bake about 20 minutes or until fruit is tender, basting once with butter mixture. Serve warm or at room temperature.

PLAN AHEAD: Prepare through Step One up to 4 hours ahead. Cover and refrigerate. Preheat oven. Uncover and continue according to Step Two.

FREEZE AHEAD: Prepare Baked Fruit. Cover with plastic wrap and foil. Freeze up to 2 months. Defrost completely in refrigerator. To reheat, preheat oven. Remove plastic wrap and foil and bake about 15 minutes or until hot.

Frozen Adobe Pie

COFFEE AND CHOCOLATE GO PERFECTLY
TOGETHER, BUT YOU COULD ALSO USE PRALINE
ICE CREAM FOR THIS DECADENT PIE .

MAKES: one 9-inch pie

- 1 pint **coffee ice cream**
- 1 **9-inch chocolate-cookie crumb piecrust**
- 1 cup **fudge sauce**
- 1 pint **chocolate ice cream**
- ½ cup **chopped toasted almonds**

  Chocolate curls (optional)

ONE Let coffee ice cream stand at room temperature for 20 minutes to soften slightly.

TWO Use a flat metal spatula or ice cream spade to scoop slices of the coffee ice cream. Line piecrust with ice cream, making a 1½-inch layer. Quickly drizzle ½ cup of the fudge sauce over the ice cream. Freeze at least 1 hour or until solid.

THREE Let chocolate ice cream stand at room temperature for 20 minutes to soften slightly. Scoop slices of the chocolate ice cream and make a 1½-inch layer on top of the fudge sauce. Quickly drizzle the remaining ½ cup fudge sauce over the chocolate ice cream. Sprinkle with almonds and , if desired, chocolate curls. Freeze at least 2 hours.

FOR ADDED SERVING FLAIR: To make chocolate swirls on each dessert plate, place ½ cup fudge sauce in a plastic squeeze bottle. Microwave on 100% power (high) about 15 seconds or until sauce is slightly warm. Squeeze decorative lines onto plates and top with a slice of pie.

Chocolate Pecan Pie

THIS IS MY DAUGHTER-IN-LAW STEPHANIE'S RECIPE, AND
NOW IT HAS BECOME A SUPER SUPPERS FAVORITE.

DESSERTS

MAKES: one 8-inch pie

½ cup butter

½ cup chocolate chips

1 cup sugar

2 eggs, beaten

½ cup chopped pecans

½ cup shredded coconut

1 8-inch unbaked pie shell
(not a deep-dish shell)

ONE Preheat oven to 350°F.

TWO In a saucepan melt butter and chocolate chips, stirring until smooth. Remove from heat; stir in sugar, eggs, pecans, and coconut. Pour into pie shell.

THREE Bake for 35 minutes (pie will be soft in the center).

FREEZE AHEAD: Bake pie; cool completely. Place pie in a freezer bag and freeze up to 2 months. Defrost completely in refrigerator.

Cream Cheese Pie

CREAM CHEESE PIE IS SO SIMPLE, YET VERY RICH AND DENSE. IF DESIRED, TOP WITH CHERRY OR APRICOT PIE FILLING.

MAKES: one 9-inch pie

- 3 eggs
- 2 8-ounce packages cream cheese, softened
- ¾ cup sugar
- 2 teaspoons freshly squeezed lemon juice
- ½ teaspoon vanilla
- 1 9-inch graham cracker piecrust

ONE Preheat oven to 325°F. In a bowl beat together eggs, cream cheese, sugar, lemon juice, and vanilla. Pour into piecrust.

TWO Bake for 30 minutes. Cool completely. Cover and refrigerate until cold.

FREEZE AHEAD: Bake pie; cool completely. Place in a freezer bag and freeze up to 2 months. Defrost completely in refrigerator.

My Mom's Strawberry Cake

MOTHER ALWAYS SPRINKLED FLAKED COCONUT OVER THE TOP AND SIDES OF THIS CAKE.

MAKES: 12 to 16 servings

Nonstick cooking spray

- 1 10-ounce package frozen strawberries, thawed
- 1 package white cake mix
- 1 3-ounce package strawberry gelatin
- 4 eggs
- 2/3 cup vegetable oil
- 1/2 cup milk
- 3/4 cup butter, softened
- 4 cups sifted powdered sugar
- 1 teaspoon vanilla
- 1 to 2 tablespoons milk

ONE Preheat oven to 350°F. Coat three 8-inch cake pans with cooking spray. Set aside ½ cup of the thawed strawberries for the frosting.

TWO In a mixing bowl beat together remaining strawberries, dry cake mix, gelatin, eggs, oil, and milk. Beat for 3 minutes, scraping bowl occasionally. Divide batter among the prepared cake pans.

THREE Bake for 20 to 25 minutes or until a toothpick inserted in center of cakes comes out clean. Cool for 10 minutes. Remove cake layers from pans; cool completely on wire racks.

FOUR For frosting, beat together reserved ½ cup strawberries, butter, powdered sugar, vanilla, and enough milk to make a spreading consistency. Frost tops and sides of cake layers.

FREEZE AHEAD: Bake and frost cake. Place in freezer, unwrapped, about 30 minutes or until frosting is firm. Remove from freezer and quickly cover with plastic wrap and foil. Freeze up to 2 months.

Cream Cheese Cupcakes

MY HIGH SCHOOL YOUTH LEADER CREATED THIS RECIPE FOR A
BAKE-OFF IN 1964, AND IT WON HER A NEW KITCHEN. THIS RECIPE
IS AS HANDY TODAY AS IT WAS BACK THEN.

MAKES: 36 cupcakes

- 3 cups all-purpose flour
- 3⅓ cups sugar
- ½ cup cocoa powder
- 2 teaspoons baking soda
- 1 teaspoon salt
- 2 cups water
- ⅔ cup vegetable oil
- 2 tablespoons vinegar
- 2 tablespoons vanilla
- 1 8-ounce package cream cheese, softened
- 1 egg
- 1 cup chocolate chips

ONE Preheat oven to 350°F. Line 36 muffin cups with paper liners.

TWO In a bowl stir together flour, 2 cups of the sugar, cocoa powder, baking soda, and salt. Stir in water, oil, vinegar, and vanilla. Fill each muffin cup half full.

THREE For filling, in a bowl beat together cream cheese, egg, 1 cup of the sugar, and chocolate chips. Spoon 1 tablespoon of the filling on top of batter in each muffin cup. Sprinkle ½ teaspoon sugar over each. Bake for 30 minutes.

FREEZE AHEAD: Bake cupcakes. Place in a freezer container and freeze up to 2 months.

Strawberry Cream Cheese Angel Food Cake

THIS IS LIKE HAVING CREAM CHEESE PIE AND STRAWBERRY SHORTCAKE ALL IN ONE.

DESSERTS

MAKES: 10 to 12 servings

- 1 8-ounce container frozen whipped dessert topping, thawed
- 1 8-ounce package cream cheese, softened
- 1 15-ounce can sweetened condensed milk
- ½ cup freshly squeezed lemon juice
- 1 prepared angel food cake, cut into cubes
- 2 cups sliced fresh strawberries

ONE Combine dessert topping and cream cheese; stir in condensed milk and lemon juice.

TWO Place angel food cake cubes in a 13×9×2-inch baking dish. Top with strawberries. Spread dessert topping mixture over the top. Cover and refrigerate.

PLAN AHEAD: Prepare up to 1 day ahead. Cover and refrigerate.

FREEZE AHEAD: Prepare as directed. Cover with plastic wrap and foil. Freeze up to 2 months.

Chocolate Sheet Cake with Chocolate Icing

THIS VINTAGE RECIPE HAS SERVED ME WELL AT A MYRIAD OF CATERING JOBS, FAMILY EVENTS, AND BAKE SALES.

MAKES: 24 bars

Nonstick cooking spray

2 cups all-purpose flour

2 cups sugar

½ teaspoon salt

1 cup butter

3 tablespoons cocoa powder

2 eggs

1 teaspoon baking soda

½ cup buttermilk

1 teaspoon vanilla

1 recipe Chocolate Icing

½ cup chopped pecans (optional)

ONE Preheat oven to 350°F. Coat a 15x10x1-inch baking pan with cooking spray.

TWO In a bowl stir together flour, sugar, and salt; set aside. In a saucepan bring butter and cocoa powder to boiling; pour over flour mixture, stirring to combine.

THREE In another bowl beat together eggs, baking soda, buttermilk, and vanilla; add to chocolate mixture, beating well. Pour into prepared pan.

FOUR Bake for 25 minutes. Pour warm Chocolate Icing over warm cake, spreading evenly. If desired, sprinkle with pecans.

FREEZE AHEAD: Bake and frost cake; cool completely. Cover with plastic wrap and foil. Freeze up to 2 months.

CHOCOLATE ICING: In a saucepan melt ½ cup butter and 3 tablespoons cocoa powder. Stir in 1 pound sifted powdered sugar, 1 teaspoon vanilla, and ¼ teaspoon salt. Add ¼ to ⅓ cup milk or enough to make spreading consistency.

Fishbowl Trifle

KEEP A CLEAR, ROUND FISHBOWL
FOR THIS FUN DESSERT.

MAKES: 8 to 10 servings

½ of a prepared angel food
cake, cut into cubes

2 6-ounce packages instant
vanilla pudding

1 12-ounce package frozen
berries, thawed

2 cups frozen whipped dessert
topping, thawed

ONE Place half of the cake cubes in the bottom of
a fishbowl. Prepare pudding according to package
directions; spread half of the pudding over the cake
cubes. Top with half of the berries. Repeat layers.

TWO Spread dessert topping over all. Cover and
refrigerate up to 4 hours.

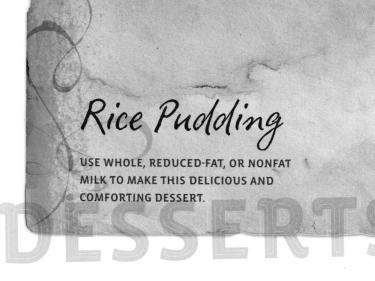

Rice Pudding

USE WHOLE, REDUCED-FAT, OR NONFAT MILK TO MAKE THIS DELICIOUS AND COMFORTING DESSERT.

DESSERTS

MAKES: 8 servings

Nonstick cooking spray

3 eggs

3 cups milk

2 cups cooked rice

1 cup raisins

½ cup sugar

1 teaspoon vanilla

½ teaspoon almond flavoring

½ teaspoon ground cinnamon

ONE Preheat oven to 325°F. Coat a 2-quart baking dish with cooking spray.

TWO In a large bowl beat eggs. Stir in milk, cooked rice, raisins, sugar, vanilla, almond flavoring, and cinnamon. Pour into prepared baking dish.

THREE Bake about 1 hour or until a knife inserted into center comes out clean.

AIOLI Garlic mayonnaise.

ASIAN FIVE-SPICE POWDER A spice blend that comes in a bottle and generally includes cinnamon, cloves, ground fennel seeds, star anise, and peppercorns.

BOK CHOY A Chinese cabbage with long, wide, crunchy stalks and tender, smooth leaves. Usually found in Asian grocery stores.

CAPERS Buds from a Mediterranean shrub cured in salt and vinegar. Used as a condiment (with dishes such as smoked salmon) or as a flavoring in many Mediterranean recipes.

CASSOULET A French stew, traditionally including preserved goose or duck, sausage, white beans, garlic, onions, and other vegetables.

CHEF'S KNIFE Also called a French knife. This is a basic, all-purpose knife used to chop, slice, and mince. The blade is usually 8 to 10 inches long with a straight back that tapers to a point.

CHIFFONADE To cut leaves into fine shreds. Leaves of vegetables or herbs are rolled into a tight cylinder, then sliced the short way, producing very thin ribbons.

COOKING APPLES Almost all apples, except Red Delicious, contain some tartness, which makes them good for cooking. The flesh of Red Delicious apples breaks down easily when cooked and becomes mushy. Other apples hold up better and keep their shape when cooked. Look for apples with rounded, smooth bases. Red Delicious apples are pointed and have knobs at the base. These are best eaten out of hand.

CORNED BEEF A brisket or eye of round cured in a brine solution. The brisket, used in corned beef and cabbage, is a flat cut of meat requiring a lengthy cooking time to become tender. The eye of round is used mostly for sandwich cuts.

CREOLE SEASONING A prepared blend of spices and herbs used to flavor Creole cooking, a New Orleans cooking style combining elements of African, French, and Spanish cuisines.

CUMIN (KYOO-mihn) Also known as comino. This spice is made from the dried seeds of a certain parsley plant and has a deep, nutty flavor. Used in Middle Eastern and Mexican cooking.

DUTCH OVEN A large, squat kettle with a lid, used for stewing and braising.

EDAMAME (eh-DAH mah-meh) Green soybeans. They come shelled or unshelled.

ENDIVE (EHn-deeve; AHn-deeve) A lettuce with large, long, stems and dark, curly leaves. Traditionally used in Caesar salad. It is larger than Belgian endive.

EN PAPILLOTE (ahn pa-pee-YOHT) A French cooking method in which food is wrapped in parchment paper or foil.

EYE OF ROUND ROAST A cut of beef round, 10 to 12 inches long and about 3 inches across. This roast is flavorful. Its shape resembles that of beef tenderloin, but it is not as tender.

FISH SAUCE A watery brown liquid made from anchovies. Very salty and stinky, this sauce adds fabulous flavor to Asian dishes and has a long shelf life.

FLANK STEAK A flat cut of beef that is flavorful but tough. To tenderize, cook rare and slice very thinly against the grain.

FLAT-LEAF PARSLEY Also known as Italian or French parsley, it has dark, flat leaves. It is preferred over curly parsley in cooking because of its smoother texture.

HERBES DE PROVENCE (AIRBES duh proh-VAWNS) A blend of various French herbs. Julia Child used the acronym STORM as a recipe for her blend, which contains savory, thyme, oregano, rosemary, and marjoram.

HOISIN SAUCE (HOY-sihn) A thick, sweet and spicybrown sauce made from soybeans, garlic, and various Asian spices. Used as a condiment or as a flavoring in Asian dishes.

ITALIAN MIXED HERBS A blend of herbs associated with Italian dishes. Usually includes rosemary, oregano, and marjoram.

KALAMATA OLIVES (kahl-uh-MAH-tuh) Dark Greek olives brined, then packed in olive oil.

KITCHEN BOUQUET A browning sauce containing a vegetable base and caramel coloring. It adds a small amount of flavor but is used mostly to give rich color.

ORZO PASTA Rice-shape pasta.

OYSTER SAUCE A thick brown sauce made from oysters, salt, and soy sauce. Used as a flavoring in Asian dishes.

PANKO (PONG-ko) Japanese bread crumbs. They are large, flat, and keep their crunchy consistency well in cooking and frying.

PLUM SAUCE Also called duck sauce. A medium-thick sauce made from fruit, vinegar, and sugar. Used as a condiment (such as a dip for egg rolls) or as a flavoring in Asian cooking.

RAITA (RI-tah) An East Indian salad made from yogurt and various chopped fruits or vegetables, such as cucumbers or bananas, and flavored with East Indian herbs and spices.

SHALLOT (SHAL-uht; shuh-LOT) A small purple onion that, like garlic, is composed of cloves instead of layers. Its subtle flavor makes it ideal for flavoring seafood dishes.

SKIRT STEAK A cut of beef from the flank. Thin, tough, and stringy, it is used mostly as fajita meat. To tenderize, marinate before cooking and slice very thinly against the grain.

SUNDAY ROASTER CHICKEN A large (5 to 7 pounds), plump chicken, bred to have an oversize breast.

TILAPIA (tuh-LAH-pee-uh) A mild, white, freshwater fish. Its sweet flavor and firm texture make it a popular choice to cook and eat.

TOASTED SESAME OIL This pungent oil is also called Asian sesame oil. It has the aroma of toasted sesame seeds and adds amazing flavor. It tends to become rancid quickly so store it in the refrigerator.

TOMATILLO (tohm-ah-TEE-oh) A fruit resembling a small green tomato but with a papery outer skin that is removed before cooking. Used mostly in Mexican cuisines.

TRI-TIP ROAST A flat, boneless cut of meat with three distinct points, from the bottom sirloin. Also called "triangular" roast because of its shape.

WHEAT BERRIES Whole, unprocessed wheat kernels. They are soaked in water to tenderize and used in salads, breads, and vegetarian cooking.

R

S

T/V/Y/Z

BRING YOUR FA~~MI~~
SUPPER TABLE

Give your family fresh, home-cooked meals—
and leave drive-through fare behind.

Super Suppers Cookbook shares the secrets
of preparing wonderful food for your family
to enjoy around the supper table. All recipes
cater to flavors your family will savor and
your need for speed.

- More than 180 streamlined recipes for
  entrées, sides, appetizers, and desserts

- Plan ahead and freeze ahead tips for
  meals in a flash

- Menus with every entrée for quick-to-
  the-table meals

- Dozens of tricks to trim time, cut steps,
  and boost flavor

JUDIE BYRD is the founder of Super Suppers, the
leader in the make-bake-and-take industry. Super Suppers
was designed to meet the needs of busy parents who want
to create quality family time around the dinner table. Judie
studied cooking at the Culinary Institute of America in Hyde
Park, New York, and Le Cordon Bleu School of Cookery in
Paris. She is a member of the International Association of
Culinary Professionals and founded The Culinary School of
Fort Worth. Her recipes have been featured in numerous
national magazines and she is a frequent guest on TV and
radio shows. Judie lives in Fort Worth, Texas.

ISBN-13: 978-0-696-23054-7
ISBN-10: 0-696-23054-2

90000

9 780696 230547

$19.95
$24.95 in Canada

Visit us at
meredithbooks.com

UPC

0 14005 23054 6